Table of Contents

In Alphabetical Order: Page:

Alive	104
Altruism	100
Animals	32
Annemarie	120
Anniversary	22
Aspen	183
Atheism	71
Audaciousness	45
Autonomy	57
Autumn	96
Averto	162
Awareness 1	27
Awareness 2	34
Beauty	60
Beethoven	30
Belief 1	10
Belief 2	198
Belonging	23
Beyond Belief	111
Bias	175
Birthdays	74
Bleeding-Heart Liberals	161
Bluebird	180
Bridges	83

	Page:
Bush Walk	197
Cake	80
Canoeing	152
Cat Haiku	177
Change	124
Civilization	190
Clover	143
Colorado Heights	179
Community	89
Competition	37
Connections	56
Consciousness 1	7
Consciousness 2	199
Cosmos	95
Costa Concordia	173
Culture	127
Death	24
Decisions	33
Dedication	193
Deep Time 1	88
Deep Time 2	204
Defensiveness	97
Derision	35
Despite	76
Dipper	168
Dismissiveness	44
Dissociation	195

	Page:
Du / You	2
Dyed-in-the-Wool Conservatives	158
Empath	135
Empathy 1	68
Empathy 2	129
Enigma	19
Envy's	117
Ephemeral	39
Epiphany	47
Essence	103
Europe	70
Evening	151
Exceptionalism	188
Existentialism	21
Expectations	41
Fairy Tales	105
Faith	36
Fall	194
Fallacy	139
Farewell	25
Father	170
Fear	12
Folly	174
Freedom	98
Friends	141
Frozen	187

	Page:
Getting Along	114
God	59
God Bless	109
Granit	86
Gratitude	14
Growth	53
Happiness	82
Hate	116
Heaven?	118
Here and Now	92
Hero	146
Hoffen / Hope	4
Holding Hands	119
Homo sapiens	147
Hubris	122
Humor	75
Ika	184
Immanence	133
I mourn	137
Impatience	164
Insight	79
Instinct	85
Irreverence	38
Islam	142
Jealousy	102
Lady	48

	Page:
Language 1	73
Language 2	101
Laughter	115
Leben / Life	5
Letters	65
Lichen	136
Life 1	66
Life 2	202
Limits of Knowledge	189
Limits of Love	178
Listening	28
Love	6
Loyalty	99
Lucidity	167
Luck	84
Magnificence	200
Manhood	186
Mantra	110
Marvel	203
Messing Up	67
Metaphysics	191
Millennium Invitation	13
Mindset	63
Mirror	154
Mistakes	201
Moment of Silence	113

	Page:
Monarch	55
Mother	205
Mountain View	182
Muddlin' Through	54
Mystery	123
Ocean	90
Oh God	131
Old Friends	157
Olduvai	49
Olympic Peninsula	171
Oneness	196
Paean for Sharlih	26
Paean to a Friend	17
Passion	140
Perfection	87
Phenotype	192
Pillow	128
Poem	163
Poetic Language	150
Poetry 1	1
Poetry 2	121
Pragmatism	9
Probability	93
Procrastination	15
Purpose	176
Pursuing Sophia	149
Ratio	69

	Page:
Rationalist	159
Regret	134
Religions	72
Relinquo	125
Respect	206
Rituals	145
Roadkill	91
Safari	153
Sail on	207
Schmupp	160
Scream	132
Security	138
Sentience	126
Silence	50
Sing	169
Sister	155
Skepticism	31
Society	3
Solutions	77
Spunky	107
Squid	108
Success	16
Supper	166
Sweat	64
Tao	18
Testament	208
That Which Counts	81

	Page:
The Good Life	94
The Promise	156
Time Spans	181
Together	130
Trauma	172
Trust 1	11
Trust 2	148
Twilight	29
Uncertainty	58
Universe 1	40
Universe 2	51
Vanity 1	78
Vanity 2	165
Wanted	106
Washing Hands	112
When!	42
Wisdom	8
Spirit, by Karl May	209
If, by Rudyard Kipling	210

Introduction

The following two hundred poems represent my more than fifty years of observations, contemplations, reflections, and sentiments on life. In no way are they complete, and some readers may not agree with one or the other. With few exceptions they are listed in chronological order.

What is poetry? I dare not try answering this question with my limited knowledge of the subject. What I *do* know, is that I like rhyme and meter. I have difficulty following narrative poetry that is lacking these two characteristics.

In ancient times, when there was yet little writing, and when peoples' myths and tales were passed on verbally through generations, it helped narrators to memorize a story if it were encoded in rhyme and meter.

I have called my collection of poems "Observations and Reflections," expressions of those things which matter to me. In addition to the following poems, I must have written more than three hundred, what I call ditties, verses celebrating birthdays, anniversaries, and other important occasions.

I composed the first poems in my early twenties when I was courting my future wife, Ute. However, after a few stumbling attempts, a long hiatus ensued with nothing more being written. During these decades life posed different challenges. Then, ten, fifteen years ago, my writing of ditties evolved into what I think are more serious poems.

Since living in Prescott, I have translated various novels, novellas, and short stories of the popular German author, Karl May. Several years ago I also translated over two hundred of Karl May's poems, most of which were written in a Christian vein. This did not prevent me, however, from tackling this difficult project. Karl May did not think highly of his poetic compositions – just as I do not of mine – but they were a means for him to express his thoughts and feelings.

His verses employ rhyme and meter, and his poems are arranged so that most are followed by Christian aphorisms. I have copied May's system in the arrangement of my poems, which are also followed and underscored by aphorisms more closely related to my thinking.

I have taken the liberty of including one of May's poems in my collection, which he wrote in 1912, left untitled, close to the end of his life. I gave it the name "*Spirit.*" Whenever I read this poem, I cannot help but be touched by May's sentiments.

And, in conclusion, I have added my favorite poem, "*If,*" by Rudyard Kipling. It incorporates all that I value in such work – content, rhyme, and meter.

Last not least, I gratefully acknowledge the editing performed by my friends, Lynn Chesson, and Zene Krogh.

Herbert Windolf   Prescott, Arizona

Poetry 1

I dabble in some poetry, in meter and in rhyme,
at times something is halfway decent,
at others – well – it's mine!
What I produce, most I call ditties,
to entertain and honor friends.
On rare occasions I do write
a ditty meant to make amends.
But most of what folks get to read,
they like and get a kick.
This is what makes my rhyming fun,
the play of words or a good pun.
More than three hundred did I write,
more will yet come, if given time.

When you don't know where you're going, it's important to
remember where you came from.
African proverb

Du

You

Rauchige Klippen,	Smoky cliffs,
harziger Duft der Pinien,	the sappy scent of pines,
Stille,	Silence,
Sonne,	Sun,
Mövenschrei,	The cry of a gull,
heisser und hungrig.	hoarse and hungry.
Sonst nichts?	Nothing else?
Ich!	I!
Und Du?	And you?

Dec. 1, 1960

Until one is committed there is hesitancy, the chance to draw
back, always inflectiveness. Concerning all acts of initiative and
creation there is one elementary truth, the ignorance of which
kills countless ideas and splendid plans:
That the moment one definitely commits oneself, then
providence moves too. All sorts of things occur to help one that
would never otherwise have occurred.
A whole stream of events issues from the decision, raising in
one's favor all manner of unforeseen incidents and meetings
and material assistance,
which no man could have dreamt would have come his way.
W.H. Murray

Society

There is I and you and he and she,
altogether the society;
but there is I and you and he and she!

Dec. 1, 1960

Was du nicht willst, das man dir tu,
das füg auch keinem andren zu.
German proverb

Hoffen

Schrecklich schön die Tage,
da man weiß.
Wissend im Ungewissen,
wartend auf morgen.
Fürchtend kaum Erworbnes
zu verlieren.
und hoffen, hoffen
und träumen.
Verdammte Ungeduld,
verdammtes Träumen.
Denk an jetzt
und vertrau auf morgen!

Hope

Terribly wonderful the days,
when one knows.
Knowing in the unknown,
waiting for tomorrow.
Fearing what barely won
to lose;
and hoping, hoping
and dreaming–
Damned impatience,
damned dreaming.
Think of now
and trust in tomorrow!

Dec. 27, 1960

So convenient a thing it is to be a rational creature, since it
enables us to find or make a reason for every thing one has a
mind to do.
Benjamin Franklin

Leben

Life

Grau in grau,
Schemen über dem Fluß,

schwarzbraun die Äcker,
hahlknorrig der Baum
und überall Leben!

Noch drei Monate
und ungestüm brichts hervor.

Gray in gray,
shadows over the river,

brown-black the fields,
bare gnarled the tree –
and everywhere life!

Three more months
and impetuously it breaks forth.

Dec. 28, 1960

The Purpose of life - a dichotomy:
In life - everything counts,
yet simultaneously - nothing matters.
H.W.

Love

Quand sera-t-il	When shall it be
le cri des mouettes	the cry of gulls
das Spiel des Windes	the play of the wind
wie Finger in deinem Haar	like fingers in your hair
a whispering of trees:	a whispering of trees:
je t'aime	I love you
ein Wissen der Trauben	the knowledge of grapes
je te bois	I drink you
Arme – golden im Sonnenlicht	arms – golden in sunlight
Sterne	stars
toi et moi	you and I
here or anywhere	here or anywhere
jamais – une fois – ou toujours?	never – once – or forever?

Dec. 27, 1960

This above all: to thine own self be true. And it must follow, as
the night the day.
Thou canst not then be false to any man.
William Shakespeare

Consciousness 1

Once consciousness was very dim,
three million years ago,
when our forebears trod the land
not different from apes.
But then this brain of ours grew,
and we learned to reflect,
a choice that animals don't have,
which makes us the "elect."
Elected stewards of the Earth,
we cover now like weed,
to make decisions good and bad,
now it's survival we must heed!
This growing brain did cost us much,
the innocence we had.
We struggled, wrestled, failed and won,
for we learned what is good and bad.
But consciousness enabled us to view the universe,
this, from its smallest to the large,
and what it means "to be."
With this capacity to see we yet barely have a clue
how it functions, how it works,
what consciousness might really be.

We seek for such evidence and appearances as are in the favour of our desires,
and to disregard those which oppose them...
We receive as friendly that which agrees with us, we resist with dislike that which
opposes us; whereas the very reverse is required by every dictate of common
sense.
Michael Faraday

Wisdom

is this precious blessing,
granted, not found by pursuit.
You must be open for its coming,
then let it grow, let it take root.
Reason alone won't get you far,
it calls for feelings on a par.
What does it give us, may you ponder:
Peace does it bring, grace,
and, yes, wonder.

We humans like to think we're rational beings. But feelings
always precede reason.
David Brin

Pragmatism

Once, many, many years ago
I came across this magic word,
so plain and yet so real.
It stayed with me throughout my life,
had import and appeal.
And without delving into it,
it was my guiding light
to find solutions, how to deal,
with all of life's contingencies.
Be practical, find out what works,
and if it doesn't, change your tack.
Thus did I work, not all was swell,
but in the end, lo and behold,
much what I did worked out quite well.

My suspicion is that the universe is not only queerer than we
suppose,
but queerer than we can suppose.
J.B.S. Haldane

Belief 1

What is belief, this wondrous thing,
that gives us strength and hope?
While we go wandering through life,
some find it, others grope.
Sure, there are many kinds of it,
some fuzzy and some bad.
Respect is due the honest ones
that are open to critique.
Well, here we go! Can this be so?
Must we not hold it true,
that which we gathered throughout life,
made us go to and fro?
Then hail to those who did succeed
to check their 'good' belief
for what be wrong and what be right
to the very end of life.

With or without religion good people can act decently and bad
people can do wrong;
but for good people to do wrong it takes religion,
the certainty to act in the name of a higher power.
Steven Weinberg

Trust 1

Once, when I crossed a parking lot
that led up to a church,
a man like me did walk it, too, to listen to a talk.
Chatting and handing him my card,
he did the same,
but when I looked,
there stood religious talk.
I gave it back while telling him:
Do save it for a worthier man!
Responding, he did ask me then:
Why don't you have some trust?
First puzzled, I gave it some thought
what kinds of trust might be?
But then, I told him my belief:
I trust –
There is no certainty!

You see, one thing is, I can live with doubt and uncertainty and not knowing.
I think it's much more interesting to live not knowing than to have answers
which might be wrong. I have approximate answers and possible beliefs and
different degrees of certainty about different things, but I'm not absolutely sure of
anything and there are many things I don't know anything about,
such as whether it means anything to ask why we're here ...
I don't have to know an answer. I don't feel frightened by not knowing things,
by being lost in a mysterious universe without any purpose,
which is the way it really is as far as I can tell.
It doesn't frighten me.
Richard Feynman

Fear

of which are many kinds,
destructive all they are.
But one that's most insidious is one that carries far.
It is the learned conviction
that dwells deep in the soul,
that one fails being good enough
to rise beyond one's "role."
It is a fear that keeps us down,
prevents from growing up,
tap the potential we do have,
does hold us back – a rotten trap.
Some people try to compensate,
are arrogant, put others down,
because their very confidence
of self is small and poorly grown.
Still others run from task to task,
from dare to dare to prove
that they are good enough – for what?
The very being that they are!
Once they have gained this bright insight,
the world does open wide.
Some baggage will be tossed aside,
their minds will soon take flight.
Lest we forget, keep in mind here:
Most that we need to fear – is fear!

I will not be afraid, because I understand.
Gentry Lee

Millennium Invitation

Since I doubt very much that we really will
be around at the turn of the third silly mille,
and in order to spite the millennium bug,
I thought to have us a chugalug,
just a little bit and to no one's dismay
down 625 Angelita way.
Get together on Friday at nine in the eve,
and calling it quits when the last one shall leave.
Now then - men and women - show you couleurs
and rsvp if you dare to be there.
There's nothing to bring 'cept your own good self
all that be needed will be off our shelf.
And if you think I'm precocious as hell,
then it's just to beat the peal of the bell.
It's not too early for'n event like this one
come on over, friends, and let's party
until this second millennium is finished and done.

To get through this life and see it realistically poses a problem.
There is a dark, evil, hopeless side to life that includes
suffering,
death and ultimate oblivion as our earth falls into a dying sun.
Nothing really matters.
On the other hand, the best side of our humanity finds us
determined to make life as meaningful as possible NOW, to
defy our fate. Everything matters.
Everything!
Robert Fulghum

Gratitude

There is this question to be "grateful" for the life
that you have had without death of your spouse
and not much trouble.
But if you don't believe in God,
who might have granted it to thee,
to whom or what are you grateful to be?
Is – was it your selfsame right doing?
Was it your fortune's lucky toss of dice?
Well, there are still some years to go,
and what they bring is not for us to know.
All we can do is to try our best
and leave to whom or what the glorious rest!
And if it should not come to be as such,
there isn't any reason for me to complain,
when I am entering, with no regrets, this other shadowy domain.

If science lost us our Western paradise, our place at the center
of the world,
children of God, with the sun cycling overhead and the birds of
the air,
beasts of the field, and fish of the waters placed there for our
bounty,
if we have been left adrift near the edge of just another
humdrum galaxy,
perhaps it is time to take heartened stock of our situation.
Stuart Kauffman

Procrastination

Some people like to postpone things
and think time might take care of them.
They may shy also from decision
or may be prone to much revision.
One other aspect enters here:
Decision made, the air is clear!
It's clear and free in many ways
and not beholden to delays.
If you are faced by any task,
it serves you best to tackle it.
Mind you, there are affairs to ponder
before you rush in, later wonder!
What's more, to keep surprise at bay,
it helps to look ahead some way.
That's why it's always on my mind:
If not ahead, I'll be behind!

Morrow, morrow, not today,
that's what all lazy people say.
German proverb

Success

is what I wish in parting
and not "Good luck," a given thing.
It does entrust the one to leave
to accomplish what he's working on.
At times Fortuna smiles on us,
at others she does not!
If mind is set to what's at task,
then why rely on fickle fate,
once in success we do believe,
then it is ours at any rate.

Behold the lowly turtle for he only makes progress when he
sticks his neck out.
Ben Bova

Paean to a Friend

What's there to give to a man of means,
who set out and accomplished what few ever dream?
Who in moments of quiet looks back what it means,
that he's passed on in life past material things.
It's ideas we inherit and pass on in life,
it's what we accomplish in joy and in strife.
It is what we stand for and teach others, too,
to generate wealth, not just making do.
And in so doing provide for others who,
did not meet those who could have told them so.
Well, then, what might one present to such a man?
Nothing material, for sure, one can.
One cannot pay back, but forward one may,
as it's been done in your name
to honor you by.
Happy Birthday, young-old Willy,
keep on going strong
and it is hoped you can still be saying:
I've done little wrong!

Mahatma Gandhi's
Seven Human Blunders:
Wealth without Work
Pleasure without Conscience
Knowledge without Character
Commerce without Morality
Science without Humanity
Worship without Sacrifice
Politics without Principle

Tao

It's claimed the Tao cannot be defined,
but may I try it after all?
I came across this statement, that of the Tao te Ching:
"When the Tao is lost there is Goodness,
When Goodness is lost there is Kindness,
When Kindness is lost there is Justice.
When Justice is lost there is Ritual.
Ritual is the Husk of Faith and Hope
and the Beginning of Chaos."
So, while it does not mention Love,
it covers quite a bit.
It's deeper than it seems to be,
what might it mean, what might be it?
What is it for the seeing?
Dare we to claim yet after all:
The Fullness of our Being!

Ritual is a bulwark against chaos in the spirit.
Poul Anderson

Enigma

Mysterious, not readily understood,
this is how I saw you,
when we met on the ship.
Names later I gave you, angels galore,
querida, Angélique, Angelita, and more.
Yet more it takes to plumb your depth,
the essence of this, your very being,
for it would take your presence and much more,
would take interaction and you seeing.
So let's probe for some time who we think we are,
yet your life is Your journey –
know that time's arrow will keep us afar.
I'm honored to be one of your 'animal' friends,
but hope, as you age, you'll make yet amends,
to find a good friend, a companion for life,
who will stick with your being
through joy and through strife.
Expect not too much, querida, my dear,
for the way we are built,
alone we are here!
Enjoy when you meet another's mind,
then be to yourself and the other kind.
Engage in this life,
of it make your best,
for the time isn't far,
when they'll put you to rest.
Now that I've said all this stuff,
which will do you no good,

I must tell you some more
to brighten your mood.
Since soon is your birthday,
your forty-sixth year,
from the depth of my heart
the best I do wish you, my very Dear;
success and much joy
for your life yet to come,
good health and much pleasure,
now be tough and then some

Fondly,
su Encandatero

If Eros, in the lines above,
does dwell a teensy bit,
Agape was the driving force,
it is her power,
she was it!

Where we have an emotional stake in an idea, we are most
likely to deceive ourselves.
Carl Sagan

Existentialism

This is why Buddha advised leaving all desires behind,
for all else would end in suffering.
But as I've said: I am, by intellect Western Man.
I must strive.
If I suffer, so be it!
In the process I learn and, hopefully, grow wiser.
I shall also overcome.
And if I'm not, then so be it.
I must accept impermanence.

Integrity is telling myself the truth. And honesty is telling the
truth to other people.
Spencer Johnson

Anniversary

When you see this cute picture
of Mona and Paul,
when ages ago they were wed,
you wouldn't believe that Mona would ever
take this youngster into her - - heart.
But there must have been something
to this Eagle Scout
that for fifty years she kept him around!
And Paul must also have found his girl great,
or we wouldn't be here to celebrate.
Now, to cut this prattle and come to the point,
we ask that you tell us a bit,
how you found each other and stuck it out,
but let's first raise a toast to it:
To this Golden Couple, who has come so far,
our heartfelt wishes, congratulations and all!
May you add many years yet, healthy and well,
you sure are a couple we all think is swell!

Trods det!
Soren Kierkegard

Belonging

I am – born German.
At home in America,
yet at heart European.
By intellect Western Man.
Human by species.
Member of all life by evolution.
Part of the universe by chemistry.

People who know little are usually great talkers, while men who
know much say little.
Jean Jacques Rousseau

Death,

this final call for courage,
when consciousness comes to its end,
when all that mattered throughout life
will now be fading and be rent.
If you did not enrich your life,
then now, it is too late!
Do not expect a heaven's gate,
nor any door to hell. –
And if some universal spirit
should take you in– this also doubtful –
it would be fine, all would be well.
Life will go on, the globe keep turning,
you're nothing but a flash of light,
but if you gave this world some purpose,
you should be satisfied, you did all right.

... what can be asserted without evidence can also be
dismissed without evidence.
Christopher Hitchens

Farewell

Now that my consciousness depart'd forever
I wish to tell you, here and now:
How much I loved you, Ute, Dearest,
but now it's time to say good bye.
In a hundred years I'll be forgotten,
and that is how it well should be,
so many others came before,
at best, I'll be a mark on the family tree.
If soul possessed me –
now gone for good –
will it linger for a while in thee?
In the hereabouts, life's deeds committed,
they had their meaning as they should.
I wish you well for years to come,
live happily and fill your life.
And when it comes to our failings:
So what! Did we not try the best we could?
I did my "things" through joy and strife,
with some regrets, as I surely should!
You stuck with me through "thick and thin,"
and in the end – lo – did we win!
But, may I tell you now in closing:
Could I have had a better wife!

The bitterest tears over graves are shed
by deeds left undone and words left unsaid.
Harriet Beecher Stowe

Paean for Sharlih

Karl – I would have loved to meet –
Did overcome his trials and tribulations.
Yet our past does always follow,
Affects and shapes and cause us sorrow.
At heart he was a decent man,
A product of his time and rearing!
Who never wronged in his life's course?
He learned from it, turned to creating!
Permit me then to quote in closing:
John 8:7, from the Book of Man:
"He who is without sin among you,
shall be the first to cast a stone."
This, I do write – a Giaur.

I do not know what I appear to the world; but to myself I
seem to have been like a boy playing on a seashore, and
diverting myself in now and then finding a smoother pebble or
a prettier shell than ordinary, whilst the great ocean of truth lay
undiscovered before me.
Isaac Newton

Awareness 1

To go through life, be unaware,
not sense what's going on;
impoverished such life does pass,
what all is missed, what might become!
To sharpen empathy for others,
be conscious of one's own beliefs,
to check one's prattling for mistakes,
be sensitive to others' needs.
But, last not least, not to forget:
that one's own needs are also met.

If you take no responsibility, you need not accept blame.
Michael Flynn

Listening

To listen well to what is said
a virtue great it is!
Most folks do filter what they hear –
provided it does even reach their ears –
through cherished, preconceived ideas.
What all they miss, it is a pity!
Like wand'rers passing in the dark of night.
But when it clicks, respect is given,
there happens, which is much too rare,
this wondrous meeting of two minds!

Chance favors the prepared mind.
Louis Pasteur

Twilight

I do these things, safari travels,
hike the great places of this land.
Yet I'm aware that all these "journeys"
will soon be coming to an end.
So, while I can, I'll do these trips,
enjoy my friends, delight in quips.
I translate books, write a bit, too,
acquired wealth to live from now.
Got a BA, did teach some courses,
and for four decades sold machines.
But I do know, the time is rife,
It is the twilight of my life.

The most dangerous world view is that of those who haven't
viewed the world.
Alexander von Humboldt

Beethoven

His work did not follow Buddhist beliefs.
He rather created the summa summarum,
the musical embodiment of Western thought,
the striving, overcoming, the triumph
of Man over fate.
His individual worth,
no matter his birth.

A human being should be able to change a diaper, plan an
invasion, butcher a hog, conn a ship, design a building, write
a sonnet, balance accounts, build a wall, set a bone, comfort
the dying, take orders, give orders, cooperate, act alone, solve
equations, analyze a new problem, pitch manure, program
a computer, cook a tasty meal, fight efficiently, die gallantly.
Specialization is for insects.
Lazarus Long, by Robert A. Heinlein

Skepticism

It is so easy to believe
for comfort, calm and for relief,
to have explained life's tribulations,
why things are as they ought to be.
But our world so complex is;
some strip it down, claim it is so!
There are these folks who do proclaim,
to know it all – no other aim.
So, when you're told something is certain,
go doubt it and be skeptical,
for what may lurk past its facade
is knowledge which these folks forbade.

Scientific knowledge is a body of statements of varying
degrees of certainty -
some most unsure, some nearly sure, but none *absolutely*
certain.
Richard Feynman

Animals

More and more we do find out
that animals have 'mind,'
and it's high time we leave Descartes,
who thought them mere 'machines' behind.
They feel, they think, they do remember,
not like a fire, but an ember.
And while they likely cannot ponder,
about their lives, in general, wonder,
they know no evil and such stuff,
instead, those that we treat with kindness,
repay it many times with love.
If we don't want to call it love,
call it self-interest, that's enough.

You see, the whole problem with the world is that fools and
fanatics are always
so certain of themselves, but wiser people so full of doubts.
Bertrand Russell

'I think.'
Addendum by James P. Hogan

Decisions

Oh, all the choices we do face
across the years of our lives!
The small stuff isn't much to sweat,
yet bigger choices must be met!
Some people carry them along,
their minds are torn by right and wrong.
What if I chose that which's no good?
What should I do, should I stay put?
Thus, they prolong exquisite torture,
not knowing what they next should do,
forever do they weigh their choices,
yet never make their minds up to
conclude salvation is so very near:
Decision made, the air is clear!

The search for truth is more precious than its possession.
Gotthold Lessing

Awareness 2

While there's awareness, empathy,
to sense what others feel,
another sense in short supply,
is seeing what goes on nearby.
To be aware of what to do,
to see what might need acting on.
Most of such "things" are piddlin' small,
while others may be rather tall.
To train oneself to seeing this,
gain the potential to affect,
is – heavens – what a word this is,
called "Situational Awareness"!

...rationality demands awareness...
David S. Landes

Derision

There are these folks who know it all,
deride their fellowmen,
as if those others were the devil's,
and surely didn't know a damn!
What is it of, they are so sure,
that they have no respect?
Or is it that their own belief
is somehow circumspect!
They often rave – it is a shame –
by which they denigrate themselves,
are not aware that what they do,
tears others and themselves down, too.
It's ugly when one hears them speak
with their aggrandizing reek.
They think they own the final truth;
is that what makes them so uncouth?

One of the biggest delusions is believing that enemies can be
destroyed by violence.
The only way to destroy an enemy totally and permanently is to
make him a friend.
James P. Hogan

Faith

What would we really be without?
it to assure us of success,
and carry us through strife and doubt.
Yet there are many kinds of faith,
the most important one which is
that we believe in ourselves
to overcome what we must face!
Then there is faith in fellowman,
faith that we do all that we can.
Faith that the Earth will keep on turning,
not to forget - faith in a higher being.
But one we must try to beware,
is blind faith leading us nowhere!

...illusions, delusions, and faith are excluded in principle and
practice
from inquiry and discovery.
David S. Landes

Competition

There are some folks who have the thought
that competition is all bad!
They feel their ethics to be better,
forgetting what life's all about.
For without strife, without competing
amoebae would not have evolved,
no Cambrian explosion would have happened,
and sure no saurian trod the Earth!
Life was tested many times
in the Perm and the Cretaceous.
Had it not been, then those who think
that competition lacks morale,
they would not have come into being,
to make that silly claim at all!

All our science, measured against reality, is primitive and
childlike -
and yet it is the most precious thing we have.
Albert Einstein

Irreverence

Why am I so irreverent
of many things, customs and people?
Yet at the same time do hold dear,
that which folks forget is here.
Irreverence is questioning, values held in high esteem,
not necessarily are they rejected,
but probed they are for what they seem.
While some irreverence is poor,
those that apply it in good measure,
there dwells quite deeply in their minds,
a reverence for all things good,
and, last not least, one for all life.

Considering the vastness and complexity of the universe
all attempts at imagining its supposed creator are
preposterous.
H.W.

Ephemeral

White does it shimmer from up north,
once more are glaciers walking forth.
The land below, still, oh so green,
soon will be losing all its sheen.
Deer, bison, elk will move down south,
bear, wolf and other creatures in their wake.
But what of man, his proud creations,
will stand against the onslaught, when
the mass of ice will grind to dust
what to the mountains it has done.
Woe to us humans – ephemeral –
not knowing, oh, how frail we are!
We will be shattered and be driven
into an unimaginable land afar.

Penned in 2008 in Jackson Hole, Wyoming.

We ... know how cruel the truth often is, and we wonder
whether delusion is not more consoling.
Henri Poincaré

Universe 1

We go our ways
like there is no tomorrow,
as if life proceeds apace.
For most people it's true,
but for many it's not,
when forces of nature strike home.
Recall the tsunami of two-thousand-four
Fukushima, the earthquake in Japan,
Haiyan, the typhoon at Takloban!
Earth will see worse of what's yet to come
that's going to strike and bring death to some.
Few people know what all happens in space –
which is that the universe is a violent place.

Is God willing to prevent evil, but not able?
Then he is not omnipotent.
Is he able, but not willing?
Then he is malevolent.
Is he both able, and willing?
Then whence cometh evil?
Is he neither able nor willing?
Then why call him God.
Epicurus, 33 AD

Expectations

To look ahead what might come true,
the joy, the benefits we might accrue,
the way some others would react,
all that we hope becoming fact.
Yet life does play by its own rules,
and people by their own!
The greatest fallacy we entertain,
is that those closest to us will behave
according to what we maintain.
Thereafter, we do feel let down
and view these perpetrators with a frown.
Great disappointment may be his,
who figures too much to come through
of expectations he held true.

The arithmetic of a lily pad placed in a pond, doubling every day, is such that it will cover the pond after thirty days. On the 29th day the pond was only half covered!
You can choose to gamble and not take action but lose the bet down the line,
with the cost being ruinous.
In ecology, as in medicine, a false positive diagnosis is an inconvenience, but a false negative diagnosis can be catastrophic.
Edward O. Wilson

When!

Beware, you people everywhere, beware the day will come,
when cataclysms strike us down, put fear in hearts of everyone.
Will it be an errant asteroid, a comet mountain-wide,
then, when it strikes the planet's face, there'll be no place to hide.
Not that it matters where it falls, on land or in the sea,
when it cuts through the planet's crust, dust will obscure the sky.
For those who live, the crops will fail, the winters will be long,
when all is over, years to go, most life will then be gone.
And if this body hits the ocean, tsunamis will rise high,
five hundred meters up, or more., to sweep what's left away.
Far inland will such waves be rushing, many thousands won't
survive,
then there are giant waves like this, from earth slides they derive.
Volcanic islands keep erupting, Las Palmas, Hawaii, and some more,
when finally such islands part, the water's surge will strike some
shore.
There are just hours from the collapse, and have you really thought,
when U.S. west or east coast will be swamped, what then will have
been wrought?
Plenty of smaller west coast slumps will come to be,
when those will happen, what little warning will there be for thee?
The polar ice caps are amelting, melt water diluting the seas' salt
content,
then, when the Gulf Stream will retreat, the shores of Europe will be
rent.
And ocean levels will be rising, beware you Tuvalus, Bangladeshi
and you Dutch,

when rising tides will swamp your shores and force you to give up so much.
Plenty of other causes may do us in, it is no question of IF.
WHEN it will happen, the one or other – that is the question – not IF.

It is worth raising an alarm about an unlikely danger, if the danger is potentially devastating.
Carl Sagan

Dismissiveness

What lurks behind dismissiveness,
a trait some people ride?
Is it they think they know it all,
or others' thoughts are not all right?
Of course, we ought to keep in mind
that there are things, right to dismiss!
But if one takes this trait too far,
there's hubris lurking and abyss!

Intolerance can harm the persecutor more than the victim.
David S. Landes

Audaciousness

Once, in a rush, I tracked a Jeep up Copper Basin Road,
paid no attention to my speed because I was in thought.
Twenty-five was there the limit, and I made it up the hill,
but when I checked my rearview mirror, I saw a cop was on my tail.
I knew I'd had it – what to do?
I pulled my car aside, took out my papers, all that stuff,
was ready for some stern rebuff.
The policeman came, I started talking:
"I'd hoped you'd follow that red Jeep!"
With him responding: "Are you German?"
A nod and – yes – I did agree.
He said: "I lived in Nuremberg,"
"That's in Bavaria," I replied,
"I am from Biebrich, by the Rhine."
He said: "I've been there, did have some wine."
"And do you know, that is in Hesse, the State my ancestors came
from.
Some came as soldiers for the British, 'sold' to them by their overlord;
to fight your forebears in your struggle of gaining freedom, which
you did!
When Washington crossed the Delaware on distant Christmas Day,
my Hessian forebears were all drunk from celebrating heavily.
Thus, Washington did have it easy, my ancestors provided it!
He had a glorious victory, you should be grateful for this bit!"
The cop said nothing, turned away, and went back to his cruiser,
there started writing – what the heck –
a chunk of money, a day's study, would likely be the pain, the
bruiser.

Then he returned, showed me his paper,
said: "You drove forty where twenty-five stood!
This time, I let you go, my friend,
the next time, though, you better be good!"

One Law for the Lion and Ox is Tyranny.
William Blake

Epiphany

At seventeen I was in Sweden,
stood on a jetty, facing west.
The sun was setting, wind was blowing,
the sea was rough – I was at rest!
I stood there for the longest time
and sang into the wind.
Then, more and more, something did happen,
wide open did become my mind.
So wide that it included all,
while I was every part of it.
I was the world, the world was I,
this, what my spirit now beheld.
A feeling was it – wonderful –
too difficult for me to tell.
How did it happen, came to being?
Much later did I understand.
It was the setting and my singing,
which so enchanted and entranced
and took me to this far-off land!

To hold on to belief come what may is a sign of religious virtue.
Contrarily, science takes it to be a virtue that one withholds
belief in the truth of a proposition until it is supported by the
weight of evidence.
Robert T. Pennock

Lady

The English language is the pits
with every woman called a lady!
There is the "lady of the night,"
the "bag" and, lo, the "cleaning lady."
Then there's the gentleman who was,
well, gentler than this ruffian ass!
Oh, what became of these good words?
which, barely a millennium old,
corrupted were they and now hold
a 'democratic', stripped-down sense,
no longer meaningful, thus hence,
'female' and "woman" should be used,
wherever that's correct to do,
not honorifics be abused!
The silliest abuse may be
when age-old mitochondrial Eve
referred was by the name of "lady"!

For every complex problem there is a simple, easy to
understand, incorrect answer.
Albert Szent-Gyorgyi

Olduvai

There is this place in Africa,
a gorge called Olduvai.
East of Tanzania's Serengetti
right in the Great Rift Valley.
The Leakey's called it 'Mankind's Cradle,"
there finding many human bones.
Well, back in nineteen-eighty-five,
we safaried there and more,
stood at the lip of this great gorge,
a local guide told of its lore.
There stood this man, in threadbare suit,
and 'lectured' to us three.
He'd worked the digs down there himself,
with the Kenyan, Louis Leakey.
This very year I had obtained my anthropology degree,
and now I heard this black man's talk
as good as at any university!
Then, when we parted and said "thanks,"
I told him,
"In the final consequence,
we sure must all be Africans!"

Learning and being taught to reason well - to be objective
and impartial - inculcate specific ideals. These are the ideals
of reason itself, and any student who does not learn them is
forever in thrall of his or her own ignorance.
Robert Root-Bernstein

Silence,

precious as can be!
Escape the hubbub, just be me.
Sit on a rock, observe the world,
way in the distance someone speaks.
Some grass blades waving in the wind,
a squirrel, noiseless, makes a sprint.
A butterfly visits some blooms,
and through the trees a titmouse roams.
There is an insect buzzing past,
a single croak a raven calls.
Now, do not think this breaks the silence,
the peace and quiet I enjoy,
oh no, it all enhances silence,
it holds me spellbound, it enthralls!

A person must be loved before he becomes lovable.
Michael Flynn

Universe 2

Once, our Universe was very small,
reached the horizon, if at all.
Then Earth was thought to be its center,
sun stars and planets to revolve about.
Until a Pole shattered this image,
from our cozy world did toss us out.
And it was found that these small smudges
spread all across the Milky Way
were galaxies past our own,
which Hubble found to fly away.
The Big Bang then explained this run,
when all there is came into being,
all matter, energy, and every sun.
Inflation it was later called,
then it was found of speeding up.
And Virtual Particles popped from the void,
to disappear again, destroyed.
Dark Matter was then postulated
explaining, among other things,
the galaxy's much faster spin.
Unseen, Dark Energy, made it's "appearance,"
explained the Cosmos' unbalanced trim.
Black Holes had long since been accepted,
with suns, all matter falling in,
but even they "evaporate,"
in years, and years, and years they fade.
Then came the thought of Multiverses,
of new ones budding from the old;

they are to be of untold numbers
their parameters varying,
some only fit for life to hold.
Quantum Mechanics is much weirder,
entanglement at distance showed.
With all this weirdness seen together,
what does the Universe still hold?
More is there yet to be discovered,
to speculate and think about.
And know, the Cosmos, we are part of,
holds more in store, yet to be found.
Sometimes, I cannot help but think,
that we are part of something great,
we'll never come to understand
us puny minds, at any rate!

What if our images of the universe simply mirror our cultural
conventions?
William K. Hartmann

Growth

All the world is wed to growth,
this, on a finite planet!
The paradigm of growth we cherish,
leads us along a slippery slope;
if we do not relinquish it,
the world we know will surely perish.
Of course, there are those many, who
do need growth for a better life;
but we, the rich, need not get richer,
there are other goals for us to strive!
Yet, people live for just today,
there's little thought what comes, what may,
until collapse brings the advice
that growth, unbridled, is a vice.
And what will take its place, what model,
that lets us grow without destroying?
If those who should be in the know
will not soon realize what's coming,
then to us will the same thing happen,
as to the rodent, yes – the lemming!

An excess of reason is itself a form of madness.
Kim Stanley Robinson

Muddlin' Through

means some success without much planning.
Is that what Nature and we do?
We improvise, as Nature does,
try something new, give it a go,
then find it needs a bit more work,
and trying we go to and fro.
So, slowly, we add to the pile,
a little here, a little there;
at last, we've gained complexity,
the Devil's goalpost, as it were!
With all this muddling, let us hope
that we'll be able yet to cope
with what is held for us in store
to muddle through a little more.

Each discovery of science adds a rung to a ladder of
knowledge whose beginning is in plain view but whose end is
not in sight - we are building the ladder as we go along. By any
measure of the ladder's height, we are closer to the beginning
of science than to its end.
Neil de Grasse Tyson

Monarch,

marvel to behold!
to cross a continent on wings,
so fragile, yet so bold.
North do they fly to Canada
two thousand miles from Mexico.
Three generations does it take,
with many victims in their wake.
A generation then, alone,
returns them to their mountain home.
There do they winter, maybe die,
yet, in the spring, again, they fly
and once again migrate in leaps,
for us, let's hope, this wonder keeps.
It's known for only thirty years,
no clue we have by which they steer.
So, should you see one flutter by
behold this wondrous butterfly.

...it does not appear that the threat of retribution is a deterrent
to immoral behavior.
Only enlightened self-interest seems to consistently produce
morality.
Edgar Mitchell

Connections

bring us ever closer,
nearby and far across the globe.
Lifeblood of our very being,
for understanding and for hope.
They do enrich, cause us to learn,
tie us together, which we yearn.
It is a joy done face to face,
or through the internet and space.
The information they supply
empowers people far and wide,
takes our worldwide civilization
onto an unknown, so wild ride.

A cultivated human being doubts. Doubt is an expression of
modesty.
Karen Duve

Autonomy

What's the importance of this word,
what it implies, what should be heard:
It calls for self-directed freedom,
with morals independent, yet responsible!
It tells us to be self-sufficient,
to tackle what comes our way;
Be able doing without others,
yet also knowing there are times,
when others know better than we may!
Be proud and humble on a par,
a mixture that will carry far.

Intolerance is the natural concomitant of strong faith; tolerance
grows only when faith loses certainty; certainty is murderous.
Will Durant

Uncertainty,

the bane of many,
too scary to be living with!
This, why we throughout our lives
shunt it away from our minds;
try, find security in rules,
in habits, customs, and beliefs.
Yet, there is no escape from it,
uncertainty is our fate!
All that we try is just disguise,
wiped off by certainty's demise.
If our life then is complete,
and without loss and sorrow, deep,
what was it we must have done right?
Were we just fortunate or bright?

Ritual is a bulwark against chaos in the spirit.
Poul Anderson

God

Most people dabble in this concept,
some do it more, some do it less.
Some, who are serious, are deserving,
some, who are taking it too far,
– despicable – they cause distress!
I have no need for this great concept,
I can't disprove it, nor affirm.
What's done through life is what's important,
this other realm might be a dream.

Religion is man's protest against the meaninglessness of
events.
Martin Nilsson

Beauty

What I will miss, when I'll be going,
will be the beauty of this Earth!
The harshness of her desert countries,
the richness of her vales,
her shores, her rivers and her lakes,
not to forget the life she bears.
So, what I've done throughout my life,
I journeyed far and wide,
took in her beauty where I found it,
across her seas and lands.
Her lakes and forests, up in Sweden,
which took me to Canadian shores;
from there to Caribbean isles
and to Galapagos, in time.
My true love, though, was Africa,
from where my ancestors bore forth,
the richness of her animal life,
which so intrigued me early on,
caused me to travel, when just twenty,
to Libya and Egypt's lore,
then to Morocco – and some more:
Stood on the plains of Serengeti and crossed Ngorongoro,
saw Moon and Venus light reflect
from her Zambezi's waters,
saw them becoming Smoke-That-Thunders,
known better as Victoria Falls.
Three days I canoed the Zambezi, like I had done before

in Minnesota and Ontario.
There was Namibia's rugged land,
the richness of the Okavango, the harshness of the Kalahari,
and a Botswana, Zim and Zambia safari.
I swam the waters of Lake Toba,
sailed the lagoon of Bora Bora.
The verdant fields of my home country –
so beautiful – brought forth some tears;
and what delight it was to see
the west coast of America.
Sequoias reaching for the heavens,
eagles cartwheeling from the sky.
The Tetons, grand, like Jackson Hole,
and north of it, the Yellowstone.
Once, the Alaskan fjords were calling,
her lands, her glaciers, wild her lives.
The mountains of New Zealand's south,
magnificent, like Doubtful Sound.
And Turkey's southern shores we sailed,
to see the ruins the ancients left.
There were the hikes in Burgundy, Provence and the Alsace,
and in the Alps, these old and civil lands,
in Tuscany and Umbria, America, and thus.
Now, in the autumn of my life,
I find experience more close-by,
in wonderful geology, so many eons old,
laid down so near my final home, the magnificent Southwest.

And come the day, if I am lucky,
there'll be a wind right strong and fast
to blow my ashes to their final rest.

Where lies the final harbour, whence we unmoor no more?
Herman Melville, Moby Dick

Mindset

Of course, we need and do believe
in something we hold true.
This something where from we depart,
and where from we pursue
the many issues of this world
to interpret and to be dealt.
But stratified a mindset is that argues ideology,
sees not the forest for the trees,
lacks any flexibility!
What is it that makes such a mind?
Is insecurity its cause, its kind?
Or is it that it knows it all
that holds it, oh, so much in thrall!

We know for certain only when we know little.
With knowledge, doubt increases.
Johann Wolfgang von Goethe

Sweat

Why do some people find it cool
not using a deodorant,
when just a little dab works wonders,
and doesn't drive some others bonkers!
Are they afraid of being hurt?
Or does "religion" play a role?
Not long ago, we, as a species,
'evolved' beyond the creature reek,
so, why do they prefer "devolving,"
and to return to awful stink?
Why then do some impose their odor,
on others with a finer nose!

...he who is without sin among you shall cast the first stone...
(meaning globalized by HW)
John 8:7

Letters

There is this collection of letters,
going back more than fifty years,
and the man and the woman who wrote them,
are now married for forty-eight years!
Full of love they are and of longing,
told, when journeys took them apart.
They describe also difficult times;
overcome, they were, in stride.
But when their material lives turned full bloom,
they drifted apart, ever closer to doom!
But memories from long ago
and reason formed the link
to pull the two, close as they were,
back from the rotten brink.
And on they went for many years
to now, in the autumn of life,
to read their letters of long ago
and refresh their enduring love.

Everyone must be who he was in the first years of his life, even
if later these were
buried under. No one can become what he cannot find in his
memories.
Jean Améry

Life 1

The other day, when I was driving
up Copper Basin Road,
an Abert's squirrel, from the right,
did try to make the other side.
It was right close before my car –
I came to a full stop.
Two cars came down the other side.
They had to see the being's frantic dashing,
back and forth, close in their sight!
I saw the creature killed already,
when it succeeded to escape,
back to my side, where I was halted,
relieved, it must have been from fright.
Why, why did these two human beings
not even slow to save this life?
Did they not see it, or not care?
What is their value for all life!

The two most valuable human characteristics: Competence
and Good Will.
H.W.

Messing Up

Once, when we were too few to matter,
the air, the water, and the land,
were able, like with other creatures,
to absorb what's left behind.
But now, six billion of one kind
and more of us to come,
we put a burden on this planet,
its air, its water, and its land.
We think we can solve our problems
with more technology and science.
Nice as the thought sounds – it is wrong.
They, and the way we're organized,
is what will get us further down.
We foul the oceans ever more,
deplete and waste the soils,
and forests that are still left standing,
for ignorants become their spoils.
Then, once we have depleted all,
a few hundred years from now,
there'll be a crash with little left
for the few of us to crow.

The Opposite of Love is Indifference.
Unknown

Empathy 1

Empathy, the sense some people have
to understand and be aware of others' feelings,
their thoughts, their suffering, their joy, their mind.
To deeply care for their experience,
and share it, not leave them behind!
This sense extends through time and space,
and bears the finest human face.

One of the biggest delusions is believing that enemies can be
destroyed by violence.
The only way to destroy an enemy totally and permanently is to
make him a friend.
James P. Hogan

Ratio,

---

reason also called,
is what should guide us in this world.
But what propels and drives us on,
are feelings and emotions.
The values we attain through reason,
which gain their power as they're felt,
we manifest in our being,
and that is fine if done with reason.

Those who invalidate reason ought seriously to consider
whether they argue
against reason with or without reason; if with reason, then they
establish the
principle that they are laboring to dethrone: but if they argue
without reason
(which, in order to be consistent with themselves they must
do), they are out of
reach of rational conviction, nor do they deserve a rational
argument.
Ethan Allen

Europe

Europe, Europe, you, my country,
born of centuries of strife;
it's for your youth to make it happen
still in the course of many lives.
To bring together all your cultures,
the richness of your many lands,
to live in peace and by just law,
open to others near and far.
Do draw them in, these other lands
and work on strengthening your bonds.
Project your values peacefully,
not to forget, responsibly!
Become a model for this world,
for other countries to behold.

We hope to see a Europe where people of all countries
consider themselves
as much citizens of Europe as of their home countries.
Winston Churchill,
three years after W.W. II

Atheism

A superior entity, a spirit or essence,
beyond our material existence
– although they may exist –
are products of our mind,
to then be believed in,
either as a comfort during one's lifetime,
or a supposed afterlife.
Beyond this,
we should remember
J.B.S. Haldane's statement
. . . that the universe is not only queerer than we suppose,
but queerer than we CAN suppose,
or, as Christopher Hitchens said:
. . . what can be asserted without evidence
can also be dismissed without evidence.

Modern science, which uses experimentation, replication of
results, analysis of cause and effect, and factual documentation
to test hypotheses, stands out as one of the millennium's most
influential belief systems.
This is a belief not in any particular theory or set of facts but in
a process through which we conduct ... the 'search for truth'.
Joel L. Swerdlow

Religions

The Hindus aren't proselytizing,
the Shintos neither do.
The Buddhists only seek Nirvana,
the Jews have troubles of their own.
Which leaves the fight for which is better,
to Christians and the Muslim spawn.
The Muslims' creed is absolute,
get in is easy, out is hard; apostasy may call for death.
But in the final consequence,
their God, the same the Christians have,
takes care of everything there is.
Their book, the Koran, is the law,
no matter that the times have changed.
The Christians, on the other hand,
are told to seek 'truth' on their own.
It makes them individuals, of which,
at least a few of them,
on revealed truth, they learn to frown.
So, which is better, time will tell,
and once the current Muslim troubles
and all the oil wealth goes its way,
and they have found themselves anew,
in a vibrant, healthy culture,
then we may say: all will be well.

Science is a system of knowledge - not a comfort.
Stepen Baxter

Language 1

is of symbols made,
words, we encode in our minds,
then, spoken, heard, they are decoded,
and, it is hoped, correctly noted.
When it does work like this – success,
yet all too often it's a miss,
for people hear that which they want,
not the transmission's real content.
It makes for poor communications,
and, what is worse, injures relations.

Being articulate is not the same as having analytical skill.
Henry Kissinger

Birthdays

From A to Z, S in between,
a dream you are – each single "one."
who are Anne, Sue and Zene by name.
And you DO span this spectrum wide,
your spirits are so rich and bright!
These days you've reached that magic number,
which you might rather put to slumber,
but, hey, what's seventy to mean,
when you have thirty yet to glean!
What fortune was it to find you!
Was it the other way around?
No matter how it came to be,
What you do bring in great abound,
brought joy to many and us too!
Enuff now, or you might get ill,
hey, what I say, is in good will.
Then, what is left for us to say:
Do have a Happy, Great Birthday!

I don't know what your destiny will be, but one thing I know:
the only ones among you who will be really happy
are those who will have sought and found how to serve.
Albert Schweitzer

Humor

A jest, a joke, a quip, a pun,
done right, are always lots of fun,
Most folks do like them, while some don't,
but then, one cannot please them all.
Outside the box one needs to think,
for quips to surface in a blink.
And all, behold – this is no ruse,
contain an element of truth.

Every good jest contains an element of truth.
Jack McDavitt

Despite

Life tosses much in our way,
for us to deal with, as we may.
Despite the worst that is to come,
we must grit our teeth – then some!
There's no alternative to grit –
to just succumb and to submit?
If everything looks dark and gloomy,
tomorrow'll be another day,
and in spite of what did pull us down,
a better future will yet dawn.

Man is a living personality, whose welfare and purpose is
embodied within himself,
who has between himself and the world nothing but his needs
as a mediator,
who owes no allegiance to any law whatever from the moment
that it contravenes his needs.
The moral duty of an individual never exceeds his interests.
The only thing which exceeds those interests is the material
power of the generality
over the individuality.
Joseph Dietzgen

Solutions

A guiding light throughout my life
has been: to find solutions.
It calls to think "outside the box,"
and not get stuck by resolutions.
It served me well and kept me limber,
and helped to broaden, this, my mind;
it taught me compromise and tolerance,
to treat my fellowmen in kind.

The prime reason for forming government has always been
to protect individuals from the violence they inflict on each other
when each is left
to face the prospect of survival as a law unto himself.
James P. Hogan

Vanity 1

Oh, Herbert-dear, what are you doing?
You write these poems, here and there.
Just as Montaigne wrote in passing,
his essays telling of his 'naked self.'
What am I doing with my ditties,
my sometimes halfway decent poems,
and other scribbles for some shelf?
It's all the same,
a bit to leave,
for after I have kicked the bucket,
or, if this sounds a trifle better,
did ride into the last sunshine.
Oh, Herbert-dear, and you, dear readers:
It's nothing really, just plain vain.

People who believe they have the truth should know they
believe it,
rather than believe they know it.
Jules Lequier

Insight

There are quite a few who believe in God,
and then there are others, who do not.
There are some who are chicken
and hang in between,
but no man religious, agnostic, or atheist
can lay claim to having seen,
that there's something or nothing
to support his claim.
It is all so futile
and a waste of time.
What cannot be known,
should be left to its own.
So, what does that make someone
not on this short list?
There is no real term:
Maybe Humanist?

Which, if any, of the many gods created by humans ought I to
believe in!
H.W.

Cake

The trails of life are full of chances,
from opportunities to choose.
But rarely is an opportunity so clear
that we not also lose.
At least some part of it we like.
It calls to weigh its pros and cons,
and to decide its worth.
Some folks decide without ado,
yet others like to eat their cake,
but – troubled – want to keep it, too!

There are no whole truths; all truths are half-truths.
It is trying to treat them as whole truth that plays the devil.
Alfred North Whitehead

That Which Counts

The world does occupy itself galore,
with problems great, beliefs, and more.
Much effort's spent in their pursuit,
the good of it is often moot!
I do not wish to, here, belittle,
the great accomplishments we've made.
But what I call for, fellow-man,
is: Be aware of your surroundings,
take action when and where you can.
Think to be kind and make things happen.
Do give a hand, signal a thank you,
Do smile, pick something up,
and, then, hold a door open, when you can.
It is the little things that count.

Beware the idealist,
for he has brought great misery upon this world.
H.W.

Happiness

is thought to be:
contentment and good fortune,
have pleasure and be satisfied,
be of good health and prosper,
not to forget the joy we find.
I cannot help but disagree
how we do happiness define,
for, is it possible for us to walk
always through life plain happily?
I'd rather think in diff'rent terms,
of fleeting, joyous, rapt sensations,
when all the world falls into place,
and we feel high in time and space.
Thus fortune, pleasure, satisfaction,
good health, prosperity and such,
will contravene the Buddha's warning
that while we live, we suffer much!
Thus constant happiness is an illusion,
at best, we can be satisfied.
But – lo – when things fall into place,
that's what I then call happiness.

Words ought to be a little wild, for they are the assault of
thoughts on the unthinking.
Maynard Keynes

Bridges

In life we cross between two worlds,
our spirit bridges the ravine.
And how we did it, note, dear reader:
What counts is what we've been.

Composed for a dental assistant while lying in the dentist's
chair,
she, wanting it for a memorial plaque on a small bridge,
crossing a gully in her yard,
the bridge given to her by her recently deceased mother.

When the Tao is lost there is goodness,
When goodness is lost there is kindness,
When kindness is lost there is justice,
When justice is lost there is ritual.
Ritual is the husk of faith and hope
and the beginning of chaos.
Tao Te Ching

Luck

I sometimes marvel at my luck,
how I survived when millions died,
came through this war with little hurt,
then lived through sixty years of peace;
this, when my parents suffered much,
lived through two wars with depravations.
Is this the luck of generations?
At six I saw Mainz going up in flames,
and during air raids in a shelter,
when frightened by the bombs' concussions,
escaped twice, helter-skelter. –
I never served in any army;
I never fought in any war.
The wealth and comfort I acquired,
cause me to marvel at my luck,
although I made it by some pluck!
But, last not least, there is no question,
it's luck we had, my generation.

Societies thrive not on the victories of factions but on their
reconciliations.
Henry Kissinger

Instinct

By cultural convention,
instinct is said "to be impelled by inner drives,"
and used to easily explain
most actions of the animal domain.
Opposed, or complementing it,
we claim for us awareness.
Now, if we travel back in time,
go ever farther down the line,
when hominins had so much less,
Erectus, Habilis, and thus,
to Lucy, Ardi, and Toumai,
with brains the size of chimpanzees.
Did only instinct drive them then and there,
or were they, after all, aware?

True science teaches, above all, to doubt and to be ignorant.
Miguel de Unamuno

Granit

Across the street lives Gran(i)t Brown,
as tough as nails, shows ne'er a frown.
Yet inside dwells a Heart of Gold,
too bad, once made, they tossed the mold!
Now he's another period older,
but darn it, he gets ever bolder!
Once more will hike this Canyon there,
which younger folks are loath to dare.
Hey, you young whippersnapper Grant,
I'm glad you are around, on hand.
So, for your eighty-third today
there isn't much for us to say:
Stay hale and sound and in good mood,
for, to your age, you'll give a hoot.
A Happy Birthday we wish you,
lots more to come,
and Joy to you.

It is a wise child that knows its own father,
and an unusual one that unreservedly approves of him.
Mark Twain

Perfection

To perfect is a sapient trait,
make things work ever better.
From knapping flint to rocketry,
from horse carts to the car,
from Lindberg's flight to the A 380,
we improved and have come far.
But whenever something fails these days,
we search for who or what's to blame,
when we, as humans, ought to learn,
that any system's bound to fail,
no matter how well it is designed and built.

Scratch the surface of most cynics and you find a frustrated
idealist --
someone who made the mistake of converting his ideals into
expectations.
Peter Senge

Deep Time 1

Some people claim we ought to live
in the present, the here and now.
I have no quarrel with this call,
beware, though, that this isn't all!
We humans are so ephemeral,
do barely think past twenty years,
when we should think in centuries,
into the future and the past.
Should we not learn to think in millions
of years, of eons, left behind,
so that we fathom our being,
so brief, of our time so blind!
For most this makes no reason and no rhyme,
but this is what is called Deep Time.

Men are so slow-witted and give themselves so easily to the
desires of the moment
that he who will deceive will always find a willing victim.
Niccolò Machiavelli, *The Prince, II, 1513 C.E.*

Community

For better or worse,
is it really a choice?
We must comprehend
that it is our fate,
if we are to survive,
we must work to become
the community of Man.
This will not require
great deeds and solutions,
but awareness and courage,
here and there, acts of kindness,
some encouraging sound.
For, believe it or not,
they do work their wonders:
it is the little things that count!

Where there is peace, there is culture; where there is culture,
there is peace.
Nicholas Roerich

Ocean

Ocean, ocean, makes me wonder,
did all this water come from yonder?
Of course, it once did come from space,
but came it fast or come apace?
Why is this Earth so well provided;
where from did all this water come?
Did Earth collect it early on,
or asteroids and comets bring it down?
And yet, the water of the three
is diff'rent in its chemistry!
So, what is left for us to ponder,
the difference and the ocean's size,
that's what is left for us to wonder.

Absence of evidence, is not evidence of absense.
Carl Sagan

Roadkill

I've caused a few myself through life,
regretted each and every one.
Occasionally, did move aside
the shattered body,
moments ago, so full of life;
an entity of rich volition,
which, in an instant found its end.
So, when I see these bodies, small and large,
ground by unthinking tires into the asphalt,
I always feel that life, so precious,
should not end thus in dust,
come to a halt.

Integrity means doing the right thing even when no one is
looking.
Jack McDavitt

Here and Now

Grant you, the present is important,
to live life fully, here and now.
To cherish every living moment,
to be aware of what we do.
Yet, there is more to being human
than living, like most creatures do, from day to day.
The past must be beheld, but also questioned,
the future must be thought of, what it ought to be.
And this not just in human life spans,
and as we usually do, in only tens of years.
No, we must learn to think in hundreds,
in thousands, even tens of thousand years.
Each of these two positions has its worth;
but living only by the former,
we will eventually face certain death.

If we hope to live a long time, we must begin to think like a
geological force.
That is, we must become the first geological force to learn to
think.
J.B.S. Haldane

Probability

We yearn for certainty in our doings,
try to make our lives work out safe and right.
Climate is meant to follow our bidding,
a hundred years to live, we might.
Yet each and every thing we do,
and that which Nature throws at us,
is fraught with upsets and with changes,
uncertainty, improbability, and thus.

No physicist ... takes seriously any of that metaphysics that
sprang up like fungus around
quantum mechanics in its early stages.
Poul Anderson

The Good Life

Science got us where we are today;
its child, technology, took part in it.
Once, when they improved our lives,
they were valued for what all they did.
Today, scientific knowledge grows apace,
much of it esoteric.
Much that they brought and bring us still,
is found obscure and even evil.
Mind you, no one should dare complain
of all the good they gave to us,
and yet, what does the future hold?
More threats, destruction, loss, and thus?
We cannot blame these Twins for all,
it's mostly what we did with them.
Growth and rapaciousness we furthered,
with all the world to follow us.
How it will end,
no one does know.
It is the future that will show!

Nearly all men can stand adversity, but if you want to test a
man's character, give him power.
Abraham Lincoln

Cosmos

As our horizons have expanded,
we're looking far beyond the pale.
We talk of Quantum Mechanics,
Dark Matter and Dark Energy,
Inflation of the universe, what was before the Big Bang,
String theory and Universal Constants,
the Multiverse, the zoo of particles that came along.
Much of this 'stuff' cannot be tested,
be not disproved, is too way out.
So, what's a simple mind to do?
Just leave it be, like I have done,
and live the balance of my life –
this doesn't impact it –
the best I can.

Science is a systematic way to avoid fooling yourself.
Gregory Benford

. . . but sometimes it takes a while.
H.W.

Autumn,

this, so glorious season,
when many colors flare alive,
and when, before the winter's onset,
Nature says: I live and thrive!
Pale grama grass waves in the wind,
leaves flutter down, a subtle hint
that winter isn't far away,
for a brief time it stays at bay.
Some birds and squirrels cache their food,
up in the sky the flocks head south,
a blustery wind tells what's in store,
but a new spring will come, for sure.

Defend your opinion only if it can be shown to be true,
not because it is your opinion.
Jack McDevitt

Defensiveness,

the bane of troubled minds.
Whatever's said, they need to weigh,
instinctively what it may say,
what's wrong with them,
day after day.
It's difficult to hear just facts,
but insecurity always impacts,
the self-assurance they do lack,
to just go on and not look back.
Lots that we hear, we should shrug off,
and know that we are good enough,
but most of all, for ourselves to love.

Whatever you have to say, make it brief
Jack McDevitt

Freedom,

to the heedless striving,
means they can do all that they want.
Yet what they miss in their pursuit,
mindless and ignorant to boot,
is, there are values to behold,
without them a society will fold.
The web connecting everyone,
of each society that works,
is slender and so quickly worn,
then, what is left, when they are done?
No, we must balance our desire,
for what we want,
with what we owe.
We lose the very thing we cherish,
if we do fail to keep this balance,
the freedom to do as we wish.

Jefferson's descendants were sucking up whatever liberties
they could and leaving
for posterity a used-up garbage dump.
Comment by Gregory Benford in *Timescape*

Loyalty

Had I been born a decade sooner,
I would have fought in World War Two.
I would have fought for my home country,
not knowing what the war was for.
Much later did I talk with men,
at war's end sixteen years of age.
But who, that old, is then aware,
what he is called for to defend?
But they were duty-bound and loyal,
and fought until the bitter end.
Years later, when they licked their wounds,
some mental, some of them for real,
they wondered: have we been defeated,
or liberated after all?
The cause they'd fought for, they now saw,
had been so wrong, so beastly raw.
But they were loyal to their country,
they did their duty, still so young.
Is it not tragic when you learn,
the cause, your loyalty was given to,
was wrong!

The two highest achievements of the human mind are the twin
concepts of "loyalty" and "duty."
Whenever these twin concepts fall into disrepute – get out of
there fast!
Robert A. Heinlein

Altruism

Why do we do something for others?
Is it that we are truly good?
Or is it that we do expect,
a thing returned, to make it up?
How could we have such selfish thought,
turn altruism on its head?
Again, why is it that we others help?
Because we feel good ourselves.

If tempted by something that feels "altruistic,"
examine your motives and root out that self-deception.
Then if you still want to do it,
wallow in it.
Robert Heinlein

Language 2

Ever changing, ever new,
yet it retains old meanings, too.
But speakers of the English tongue,
they are so careless, often wrong,
and not aware of what they do,
don't give their language proper due.
They do pronounce kilOmeter,
which makes it then millImeter!
And would they know the difference,
between mIcrometer and micrOmeter?
A group of people of mixed gender,
has been reduced to: "Hey, you guys."
And asking someone: "How are you?
They'll tell you: "I'm good."
I often jokingly ask then: "Which way"?
Ah well, it's only language that's perturbed and in dismay!

The growth of knowledge depends entirely on disagreement.
Karl Popper

Jealousy

What's jealousy, this powerful feeling,
destructive to the one possessed.
It strains the mind, makes insecure,
the one who falls to this emotion.
It tries to hold on or to gain,
that which's so difficult to chain.
It wastes much energy, so precious,
that's better used to stiffen mind,
or should that fail,
to just let go.

A competent and self-confident person is incapable of jealousy
in anything.
Jealousy is invariably a symptom of neurotic insecurity.
Robert A. Heinlein

Essence

What I have written is but part,
what could be said about the world,
about each subject, large and small,
and there is much yet to be covered,
and much that wasn't touched at all.
If there is time, more may be heard,
if not, it is my final word.

Don't try to have the last word.
You might get it.
Robert A. Heinlein

Alive

They come in all sizes,
large, medium and small,
in many a color,
in boisterous shapes,
so bright and alive,
and I love them all!
So, what are you wond'ring,
my reading friend?
It's not what you think!
It's Zinnias, I meant.

A man is known by the quotations he keeps.
Old Scottish proverb

Fairy Tales

When I was four, and dusk was settling,
my grandma took me on her lap.
She told me fairy tales galore,
for me to grow up with this lore.
In fairy tales all things can happen,
like magic, coming from a void.
Impressionable, as kids are, I took it in, believed it all.
Feats the heroes did perform
came out of nowhere, as a norm.
No matter, physical or mental,
they happened on their beck and call!
I ran with it, made them my own,
subliminally believed it all.
Then, when I got into my teens,
I thought I had these very means,
to do, like magic, what I wanted, at any time, at any call.
That tasks of physical and mental nature,
called for my nose to the grindstone,
I, by the hard way, had to learn; it doesn't help to simply yearn.
Thus, in the many years to come,
I buckled down, worked, and then some.
But faintly, back, deep in my mind,
there's still that voice that whispers on,
that I can do whatever comes,
like magic, on my beck and call.

It is the mark of an educated mind to be able to entertain a
thought without accepting it.
Aristotle

Wanted

We enter this life;
alone we are.
We seek the one,
who,
not just in part,
but as a whole,
is going to want us,
body and soul.

Invictus
Out of the night that covers me,
Black as the Pit from pole to pole,
I thank whatever gods may be
For my unconquerable soul.

In the fell clutch of circumstance
I have not winced nor cried aloud.
Under the bludgeonings of chance
My head is bloody, but unbowed.

Beyond this place of wrath and tears
Looms but the Horror of the shade,
And yet the menace of the years
Finds, and shall find me, unafraid.

It matters not how strait the gate,
How charged with punishments the scroll.
I am the master of my fate:
I am the captain of my soul.

William Ernest Henley

Spunky

Twelve years ago, we got a kitten;
we found her at the local pound.
Lively, she begged us: "Take me, take me!"
and in an instant we were smitten.
We soon found that this 'character'
had 'personality' like none before.
Self-assured, she knew her worth,
and yet, as sociable she is,
we could not help, this little being, to adore!
Without a leash, we daily walk the yard,
which she does ask for with assurance,
and she will come to us when called,
although, if there is something holding her attention,
return may be a little stalled.
And sometimes, of her own volition,
she makes a beeline towards us,
to find acknowledgment of this, her being,
which we are happy to extend.
And when it's time to go inside,
meows and hisses do us chide,
while this, to you, sounds uppity,
it's not for nothing that we called her Spunky.

The cat could very well be man's best friend
but would never stoop to admitting it.
Doug Larson

Squid

Once, snorkeling in clear tropical waters,
I met some squid, correctly, only two.
There, we hovered in the water,
observing ourselves – what show!
The two flashed iridescent signals,
their meaning I was wont to know.
I couldn't help but think and wonder
what these creatures thought of me.
They showed no fear in all their beauty;
but me, unable to flash back,
they left, for better things to see.

The eye sees only what the mind is prepared to comprehend.
Henri Bergson

God Bless

I wonder when the President,
giving a speech – coming to its end –
will then conclude it with, when all is told,
"God bless America –
and all the peoples of this world!"

All evil and good is petty before Nature.
. . . there is a Universe to admire that cannot be twisted to
villainy or good,
but which simply is.

Vernor Vinge
in: *A Fire upon the Deep*

Mantra

"The People" are supposed to know
what's good for them, the Then and Now.
Watchword of politicians, pundits, and their cronies,
they keep repeating this – these phonies!
They surely know – the people, mostly,
think only of the here and now,
but rarely see the consequences
and less the roots of this great show.
It is elites, its leaders, who can look ahead,
make the, at times, painful decisions it does take,
or state and rule – if wise – what is to come in time,
like what the Founding Fathers had in mind.
So, quit this mantra of "The People,"
that they make choices, good and right.
It takes good leaders and decisions
to gain a future safe and bright!

When a society no longer works smoothly,
respect for the established order decays,
the underlying mystique disintegrates,
and chaos and suffering follow.
Poul Anderson

Beyond Belief

One way or another, people believe
in a god, no god, an afterlife or rebirth.
Lots more are around to hang your hat on.
Agnostics are those who don't know which's the one.
But whatever's the belief – means not knowing at all.
Then why not stop diddling,
and of whatever it is be no longer in thrall?
For what cannot be known
is Nothing to ponder;
we ought to dismiss it
and leave it alone!

"Deny God and you are doomed to spend your life searching
for Him,
if only for the sake of finding out whether you're right
about His nonexistence.
And if you neither deny God nor accept Him, what then?
Wouldn't you then be a truly simple person?
I suppose you would, yes.
But I'm yet to find any person like that."

Robert Silverberg
in *The Face of the Waters.*

Washing Hands

With so many people and bugs on the prowl,
it's easy to run of the latter afoul.
And as paranoid as we have become,
we keep hearing "Wash hands!"
which way, for how long, how thorough, then some.
This is fine as it goes,
but it shouldn't be all,
for between all this washing,
what people do,
they are rubbing their noses, their eyes, the mouth, too.
No one has warned them,
and they aren't aware,
this is how they transfer
the bugs they have picked up, in between, from somewhere;
from doorknobs and handles, from bank notes and counters,
from keypads and whatnots, whatever is there.
So, keep off your noses and eyes to beware!

He's a Blockhead who wants a proof of what he Can't
Perceive.
And he's a Fool who tries to make such a Blockhead believe.
William Blake

Moment of Silence

There was this day when I'd been invited
to join a gathering of twenty-five;
submariners they were of old and new;
a few of them had brought their wives.
The reason for my presence was
that I'd translated the account
a German U-boat man once penned.
The gathering went through its paces,
yet, when I looked at all the faces,
I wondered when one of these people,
Americans, all of them were,
would ask for a "Moment of Silence,"
for the 3,000 who had died that morn',
the eleventh of September of two-thousand-one.
The request never came, which I
– the foreigner and guest –
felt inappropriate to voice.
So, to this day, my conscience haunts me
that I had not the guts to ask!

Regret for things we did, can be tempered by time;
It is regret for things we did not do,
that is inconsolable.
J.D. Lewis, Cadet, USAFA '98

Getting Along

We are creatures of many persuasions,
beliefs, and wishes, and what not,
of hate and love and altruism,
jealousy and greed and hope,
with irrationality and reason added to the lot.
It's thus a marvel to behold
that we have come so far, all told,
as individuals, as groups and nations
and have, so far, not killed us dead.

I have seen these contradictions and they have not
rebuffed me.
Jean Jaques Rousseau

Laughter,

sign of joy, delight, or pleasure
is, of manifold expressions,
one of our greatest treasures.
Ranging from giggles to loud roars,
it is great fun to make it happen.
A quip, a jest, or a quick pun
will cause an uproar, if well done.
It adds to our social fabric,
connects us, when not mean of spirit.
So, when you cause it, keep in mind,
make sure to do it good and right!

If a dog jumps in your lap, it is because he is fond of you;
but if a cat does the same thing, it is because your lap is
warmer.
Alfred North Whitehead

Hate,

is a word so strong in meaning,
yet people use, abuse, and do demean it,
when saying "I hate this," a trifle.
Shame on their language,
when "dislike" is truer,
when "hate" should be reserved –
for what?
Be warned – we only "hate" by far,
that which is stronger than we are!

It's a strange world of language in which skating on thin ice can
get you into hot water.
Franklin P. Jones

Envy's

such a troubled feeling,
the painful want for what another does possess.
Is not the envier aware
that his position – as it were –
must be inferior to the one possessing?
Poor schmuck, possessed of envious feelings,
that serve him only if he works
to get to where the other made it,
or be consumed by his poor spirit.

You can't get ahead while getting even.
Dick Armey

Heaven?

Questions abound
that cannot be answered,
which is why we should leave them be!
Like why we are here,
and have we a purpose,
where do we go when we die?
If we go anywhere!
For those of the faiths,
they have all the answers,
but once the doors close,
there will nothing be.
The universe 's too big to bother
about us midges here.
So while not away the time you are given,
use it here, and now, and well!
For when you are dead,
nothing's going to happen,
for there ain't no heaven,
and there ain't no hell –
except for the one we create ourselves!

There's a distinction between "known unknowns," the things we
know we don't know,
and "unknown unknowns," the things we don't know we don't
know.
Black Swan Idea, popularized by Nassim Taleb

Holding Hands

In the night
she lies next to me.
I reach out with my open hand
and quickly hers comes touching mine,
probing, playing, firmly resting.
My fingers caress,
hers padding back.
What trust she extends
to me holding on.
In touch with another being,
we enjoy its pleasure.
I'm holding hands –
with a cat.

Way down deep, we're all motivated by the same urges.
Cats have the courage to live by them.
Jim Davis, creator of "Garfield."

Annemarie

A kindred spirit I have found
whose poems, manifold, abound.
A joy it is to find so late,
in life – behold – a dear soul mate.
I thank you for your words, so kind,
your understanding of my mind.
And if some subjects make us differ,
we keep the arrows in the quiver,
for both of us, I think, agree,
that variation is life's creed.
Whatever comes, I wish you well,
a healthy life, and many years,
with much to write and much to tell.

We think few people sensible except those who agree with us.
La Rouchefoucauld

Poetry 2

is a means to me
to tightly express
how things ought to be,
or how they are
when carried too far.
Not that I know
how all things ought to be;
I just give it a shot
for others to see.
And should I be wrong,
does it matter a lot?
At least I did manage
to stir up the pot.

I believe that ideas such as absolute certitude, absolute
exactness, final truth, etc. are figments of the imagination
which should not be admissable in any field of science...This
loosening of thinking seems to me to be the greatest blessing
which modern science has given us. For the belief in a single
truth and in being the possessor thereof is the root cause of all
evil in the world.
Max Born

Hubris

is my concern
to reach beyond
that which we are capable
of handling
safely
To reach for the stars
maybe
or maybe not
is our fate
to find out

We've arranged a global civilization in which most crucial
elements profoundly depend on science and technology.
We have arranged things so that almost no one understands
science and technology.
This is a prescription for disaster. We might get away with it for
a while, but sooner or later this mixture of ignorance and power
is going to blow up in our faces.
Carl Sagan, in The Demon Haunted World; Science as a
Candle in the Dark

Mystery

From where came the universe,
and how will it end?
Questions we've pondered,
without answers, to no end.
Heat Death is looming,
we seem to be sure,
but what will come after
and what was before?
How it came into being,
with or without Big Bang,
did it bud off a Multiverse without end?
It's all speculation,
doesn't answer a lot,
especially the question
why there's something
instead of not.
Since this is the question
we can never answer,
it leads some of us
to name a creator.
This, too, speculation,
we should leave it be,
it being the Greatest Mystery.

Why is there something instead of nothing?
Plato, Aristotle, Thomas Aquinas
(the Argument from first Cause)

Change

is the conservative's bane,
who never would like to see anything wane,
of which they grew fond,
or what's supposed to be "so,"
as if life were static
and never grows.
Yet life's destiny is to forever change,
for, if that weren't so,
dinosaurs would still range.
There are rules to hold on to,
but others to fade.
Don't forget all that man has made!
With the changes we make
in how we live,
conservatives should know
this requires some give.

A conservative is a man with two perfectly good legs who,
however,
has never learned how to walk forward.
Franklin Delano Roosevelt

Relinquo

means "to leave behind" and also "to leave be."
Its Latin root appears in English
in closely related "to relinquish."
You may now ask me, dearest reader,
why you should heed a Latin word?
Well, mankind has, for ages long
pursued what gods there be,
and to this day, how plentiful,
has come up with three thousand and three.
A few are "greater" than the others,
but all are products of man's mind.
Be certain, more will come in time!
So, whether there be a creator,
we folks can only wonder;
and whether there is truly none
is useless to behold and ponder.
So many beliefs are held by man,
like atheist, agnostic, theist, deist, and so on,
but why go on with all this grist,
and call one who did leave behind
and focused on the daily needs,
to coin a new word –
a Relinquist.

I must not fear. Fear is the mind killer. Fear is the little death that brings total
obliteration.
I will face my fear. I will allow it to pass over and through me. Only I will remain.
Frank Herbert of "Dune"

Sentience

What is this thing called sentience
providing insight to this world?
How deep, how broadly is it spread,
among the creatures, far and wide?
Bacteria floating in the seas
know how to move towards the light;
a mouse knows to avoid a cat,
a tiny creature, not too bright.
Crows stash their seeds for winter come,
find them again, except for some.
Innate behavior we call this,
reserving sentience for us.
Awareness runs among all beings,
with some it's less,
with others more.
We should acknowledge and respect this feature
because among us walk so many,
whose awareness, sentience, is of poor nature.

Some things have to be believed to be seen.
Ralph Hodgeson

Culture

*is supposed to be
the hallmark of humanity.
But what of creatures, large and small,
who, more or less,
own this behavior after all?
It's only in these recent times
that we have learned enough to say,
that we are not alone encultured,
but share this feature with a few.
So, let's step down from our height,
give credit to those due,
treat them humanely
as becomes us,
and let this hallmark become true!*

Man has stone-age feelings, Middle Age institutions, and a
god-like technology.
Edward O. Wilson

Pillow

My arm rests on a pillow
elaborately stitched.
It once came from India,
bought by my gone sister-in-law.
The years have caused it to fade a bit,
but I often wondered of who stitched it?
It was likely a woman,
poor as a mouse,
who worked for a wage
not enough for life.
Many times have I thought:
I'd love to meet her,
to tell how I admire her work.
But most likely she's long gone,
to where no pillows are made.

Millions long for immortality who do not know what to do with
themselves on a rainy Sunday afternoon.
Susan Ertz

Empathy 2

To feel, to sense what others feel,
and when from suffering they reel
from shortages and hurt or pain,
to feel for them is all the same.
And feeling empathy for people,
one can with creatures large and small,
with mountains, seas, and, too, the planet,
in short, it's possible to love them all!
How does this sense arise in some,
while others couldn't give a damn?

Those who dream by day are cognizant of many things that
escape those who dream only at night.
Edgar Allan Poe

Together

Whenever life's been good for awhile,
there seems to arise that itch,
to let things slide,
only think of one's self,
with people and nations forgetting that before
a number of things were not as rich.
New generations never knew or forget,
what troubles there where,
what there wasn't or missed.
If only there were then people who'd shout and hail:
"Together we rise or together we fail!"

What all the wise men promised
has not happened,
and what the damned fools said
has come to pass.
Melbourne

Oh God

I love to jest, make a good pun,
my wife then comments, when I'm done,
often, but not across the board:
"Oh, my god,"
to which I retort:
"That, I am not."

Our greatest glory is not in never failing, but in rising every time
we fail.
Conficius

Scream

The are moments, diffuse,
when I feel I should scream
in anguish about things that are
and have been.
Things that are happening,
I'm powerless to change,
which is why I feel,
to raise head and hands
high up to the heavens,
and give voice to my feeling,
this primal urge to scream.

Is God willing to prevent evil, but not able?
Then he is not omnipotent.
Is he able but not willing?
Then he is malevolent.
Is he both able, and willing?
Then whence cometh evil?
Is he neither able nor willing?
Then why call him God.
Epicurus, A.D. 33

Immanence

Oh, what people believe –
that transcendence there be.
The surprise they will have
when they get there and see,
that there's nothing at all
what they imagined to be.
We are of this earth
and return we will.
Make the best of your stay,
while you're able still!
Live within the experience
of what you can know,
and leave what's beyond
to those imagining to know.
And once all's been said,
and all has been done,
tranquility be your goal
for the final run.

All things being equal, the simplest explanation is to be
preferred.
William of Ockham, 1280-1347
Occam's Razor

Regret

We are all children
with parents, too.
Most carry issues,
that's for sure!
Some do address them,
others do not,
some keep them through life –
the whole damn lot!
Try to resolve them
while you can,
for life – rest assured –
is going to end.
My issues – long solved –
left regret for what happened,
for what did not,
and for what might have been.

I was angry with my friend
I told my wrath, my wrath did end.
I was angry with my foe:
I told it not, my wrath did grow.
Songs of Experience, A Poison Tree.
William Blake

Empath

How often have I wished
to access the mind
of my cat, other animals,
not of my kind.
To understand what they think,
what they want us to know,
what is truly meant
by my cat's meows.
I wish not to enter
the minds of men,
for we have language
to commune with our ken.
Oh, how often have I wished
to also be ken,
to my fellow-beings,
with little language to tell.

It is not what we eat but what we digest that makes us strong,
It is not what we read but what we remember that makes us
wise,
It is not what we earn but what we save that makes us rich,
It is not what beliefs we hold but what we do with those beliefs
that make us what we are.
Old Chinese misquotation.

Lichen

There, on the kitchen windowsill,
rests for the past few years,
brought from Wyoming's Jackson Valley,
a fist-size rock, covered by lichen,
of various colors and kind.
Dead do they look,
these symbionts of algae and fungi,
yet hardy live they on.
From time to time,
I love to feed them,
let water run over the rocky rim.
It is amazing how they "drink,"
take in the water of life.
It is a joy to care for them
and keep these tough beings alive.

When beggars die, there are no comets seen –
The heavens themselves blaze forth the death of princes.
Wm. Shakespeare

I mourn,

I grieve,
and I rage against fate,
for the lives lost in the Yarnell fire,
of nineteen men in the prime of life,
men who only days earlier had protected our town.
And now their horrible deaths,
scorched, incinerated by fire,
in the shelters they sought,
insufficient, for naught.
Their families bereaved,
their children alone,
Prescott will gather,
to act for what little can be done.

All Nature is but art, unknown to thee;
All chance, direction, which thou canst not see;
All discord, harmony not understood;
All partial evil, universal good:
And spite of pride, in erring reason's spite,
One truth is clear; whatever is, is right.
Alexander Pope
"Essay on Man, Epistle I"

Security

Since time immemorial
our species has tried
to provide security,
as far as we might.
We did succeed,
quite well, one might say,
but Nature is fickle,
keeps testing us,
try as we may.
The Universe does not care,
one way or another.
It's a violent place,
of which few are aware,
until we are struck,
out of blue sky,
only to learn
that we aren't much better
than an ant under foot.

. . . survival is Nature's only form of flattery.
David Brin

Fallacy

As it stands today
with our instant communication,
we learn within hours
of events far away,
worldwide, in pictures and word,
with the emphasis always
on catastrophes and murders,
on killings and wars,
on deaths and deceases,
as if that were all!
This will lead us to think
that there's nothing but evil,
nothing but suffering,
and only ill will!
Beware, dear watcher,
listener to such:
While truly there is plenty of evil,
there's also goodness –
so very much!
It would be fallacious to dwell just on evil,
do keep in mind that much good
works in silence!

What nature doesn't do to us,
is done by our fellow man.
Tom Lehrer

Passion,

easily aroused,
impulsiveness,
too poorly checked,
kept our forbears down and back.
It is one reason
why it took millennia
for our species to mature
to form cohesive groups,
not just endure.
By curbing impulse when it's needed,
we have been able to form nations,
cooperate for the common good.
And those of us
who groom this feature,
as individuals and as a group,
do reap its benefits,
and what is more –
evolve towards a better nature.

If we could read the secret history of our enemies
we should find in each man's life sorrow and suffering enough
to disarm all hostility.
Henry Wadsworth Longfellow

Friends

of my younger years
lost over time.
Some married, some moved overseas,
some died before their time.
Now, in the autumn of my life,
I wonder what happened to them,
how they survived?
Who might be alive;
how did they fare?
How did they treat life,
how did life in return?
I have checked and checked,
found one here and there,
but by far not enough
to be pleased,
as it were.
How good would it be
to trade our lives,
to talk of what made us,
at what we succeeded,
and what hurt
while we strived.

You only live twice:
Once when you are born,
and once when you look death in the face.
Basho, Japanese poet, 1643-94

Islam

whose very name means "Surrender to God,"
is absolute – total – objection is mute!
Apostasy is threatened with death,
and denial of God is a matter no less.
What is one to make
of strictures so tight?
What of its claims for tolerance, one might?
Until the cultures adhering to it –
with customs even enshrined in their faith –
have separated religion from state,
and acknowledged this separation as truth,
not one will succeed in the course of time
and be able to maintain a democratic mandate.

Nobody ever did anything very foolish except from some strong
principle.
Melbourne

Clover

There once was this svelte young woman,
who could pick four-leaf clovers on request.
She would look in the grass,
bend down, and pick one,
– endearing and sweet –
which made her feel close to my chest.
And lo and behold,
when all is told –
she married me,
surely at the clovers' bequest.

To laugh is to risk appearing the fool.
To weep is to risk appearing sentimental.
To reach out is to risk involvement.
To expose feelings is to risk exposing your true self.
To place your ideas and dreams before the crowd is to risk
their love.
To love is to risk not being loved in return.
To live is to risk dying.
To hope is to risk despair.
To try is to risk failure.
But the greatest hazard of life is to risk nothing.
The one who risks nothing
– does nothing
– has nothing
and finally – is nothing.

He may avoid sufferings and sorrow,
but he simply cannot learn,
feel, change, grow, or love.
Chained by his certitude, he is a slave;
he has forfeited freedom.
Only one who risks is free.

Anonymous

Rituals,

societies need,
for coherence,
perpetuation,
and the values they heed.
I don't question their purpose,
but it gives me a chill,
whenever I'm exposed to a ritual's will.
No matter whose anthem,
no matter the cause,
my individuality, my independence,
become subsumed
and I muse:
What is it that I'm afraid to lose?

In Germany they came first for the Communists, and I didn't
speak up because I wasn't a Communist.
Then they came for the Jews, and I didn't speak up because I
wasn't a Jew.
Then they came for the trade unionists, and I didn't speak up
because I wasn't a trade unionist.
Then they came for the Catholics, and I didn't speak up
because I was a Protestant.
Then they came for me, and by that time no one was left to
speak up.
Martin Niemoeller

Hero

A word which these days,
more often than not,
is used wrongly, abused, debased, and what not.
Just as every woman
today, in this culture,
is so readily seen, as being a lady,
when her manners – behold –
do not merit such esteem.
Too many people
who just do their jobs,
are today called heroes,
when they are not.
America,
don't become awash in heroes,
when ordinary people
perform extraordinary deeds.
Keep misusing this word
and we all become heroes,
with the language
reflecting the sense of its users.
There are true heroes,
let's keep this in mind,
who risk their lives,
for their fellow-kind.

Fondly we think we honor merit,
when we but praise ourselves in other men.
Alexander Pope

Homo sapiens

Wise Man, we call ourselves,
as if we were such.
It serves to distance us
from other creatures,
to lord it over them,
to feel better, thus.
But the way we behave
and interact with each other
– I sometimes think –
we haven't got what it takes
and act much more like glorified apes.

. . . my experience of men had long taught me that one of the
surest ways of begetting an enemy was to do some stranger
an act of kindness
which should lay upon him the irritating sense of an obligation.
Samuel Clemens

Trust 2

engenders information,
which, exchanged, increases trust.
Trust, in turn, will lead to caring,
tended well, to everlast.
Those distant from this interplay
are unaware of what they're missing,
will evermore fall short in life,
be it of trust or be it caring.

He that leaveth nothing to chance
will do few things ill,
but he will do very few things.
Halifax

Pursuing Sophia,

tongue-in-cheek,
but seriously – it's what I seek!
As if one could pursue sophia.
There are the followers who need a leader,
for that which they are wont to find.
Behold, it must be found within,
and must evolve in every mind.
Is wisdom not a precious gift,
bestowed onto the one who's open,
to learn, search, tolerate, and to forgive,
forget, and ponder, reject, sift,
but who will not forget to live?
Then there are love, and grief, desire,
compassion, equanimity to forge.
The rational and spiritual need balance,
uncertainty must be accepted,
with knowledge surely circumscribed,
all blended into a unified whole.
And in the end, will it bring peace,
a distance from the daily race,
become subsumed into the fading light,
enter oblivion, neither dark nor bright?
Then I – a nothing – one with the world.

Learning is the best of all wealth;
it is easy to carry, thieves cannot steal it,
tyrants cannot seize it; neither water nor fire can destroy it;
and far from decreasing, it increases by giving.
Naladiyar (ca.5th-6th century) Tamil ethical literature

Poetic Language

Once when we cruised Alaskan fjords
of stark, yet sublime sights,
there were thin wispy clouds suspended
low, before the mountain sides.
A guide we asked:
"What are they called?"
was quick, and smilingly replied
"It's Dragon's Breath,
that comes to mind."

Only an earth dream.
With which we are done.
A flash of a comet
upon the earth stream.
A dream twice removed,
a spectral confusion
of earth's dread illusion.

Edgar Lee Masters

Evening

The day is closing;
I sit on the deck,
gaze toward the mountains, the Bradshaws, east.
Dusk is settling,
bats take wing, crickets chirp,
the air turns chill.
The last of the hummingbirds comes to sip
before it settles for its nightly sleep.
Phainopeplas make a final dash
up into the sky for insects to catch.
Some dogs still yap until all falls still.
The heavens darken, the first stars appear.
There shines Vega in Lyra
and Deneb in Cygnus, Altair in Aquila,
in Ursa Minor, Polaris.
At last comes Delphinius, a small constellation,
tiny compared to Sagittarius
with its "Teapot" configuration.
At times a satellite moves serenely across,
the occasional meteor is a lucky toss.
Then comes the time to join the hummer
and retire to a pleasant slumber.

The most beautiful thing we can experience is the mysterious. It is the
source of all true art and all science.
He to whom this emotion is a stranger, who can no longer pause to
wonder and stand rapt in awe, is as good as dead: his eyes are closed.
Albert Einstein

Canoeing

We plied the waters of Quetico,
up in the wilds of Ontario.
Dropped off by float plane
in the midst of nowhere,
we enjoyed the solitude
with wolf and bear.
Not that we saw them,
too shy they were,
but saw their marks when we portaged,
heard their howls from afar.
And blueberry season
was a joy, all told,
the water pristine,
to drink pure and cold.
The fishes were tasty,
the mosquitos bold,
but I do not complain
of such paradise to behold.

Oh, how desperately bored, in spite of their grim determination
to have a Good Time,
the majority of pleasure-seekers really are!
Aldous Huxley

Safari

in Swahili means "long journey,"
and I traveled thus a number of times.
Safaris took me to Kenya and Tanzania,
to Botswana, Zimbabwe and Zambia's wilds.
To walk the bush,
canoe the Zambezi,
never knowing what I would come across,
buffalo, lions, a herd of impala,
elephants, a hippo, or a croc,
returned me to the beginning of time
when our forebears walked this land.
The sense of danger was sublime,
knowing I was a creature of many,
potentially a victim of any.
A tamed environment has been my home,
yet Africa's savanna felt like a second one.
So, when I once told this to another man,
who knew Africa for a hundred times,
he, with a straight face, said to me:
"It is genetic memory."

We shall not cease from exploration
And the end of all our exploring
Will be to arrive where we started
And know the place for the first time.
T.S.Eliot

Mirror

Mirror, mirror, on the wall,
who am I to tell it all?
If I have learned some things to tell,
it's minimal to what there is,
and calls for silence just as well.

Our knowledge can only be finite, while our ignorance must
necessarily be infinite.
Karl Popper

Sister

I once had a sister,
a good-looking woman.
But she never married;
I don't know why she tarried.
Hannelore was her name.
From age sixteen she smoked
cigarettes – what a shame.
I often asked her to quit this addiction,
and she always said to me:
"When the doctor tells me to quit,
I will follow his advice,
just wait – you will see."
But when the time came
that the doc said "stop,"
a lung was cancerous and had to come out.
A year after that she passed away
at age forty-seven,
way too young, I should say.
There are days,
twenty-two years on,
when I miss her much,
only brother that I am.

Procrastination is the thief of time:
Year after year it steals, till all are fled,
And to the mercies of a moment leaves
The vast concerns of an eternal scene.
Edward Young

The Promise

As far as we've come,
with all we've accomplished,
we also have messed up good!
We degraded the oceans, the lands and the air,
ignorant of what we were doing,
or did not even care.
But now that we've become aware,
how we befouled our planet,
we find ourselves at the cusp of change,
a host of means and developments
may presage a brighter future,
when technology more benign
will rein in excesses
for a better time.
Have we learned enough
to change our ways?
Will we do our best
no longer to befoul our nest!

Any sufficiently advanced technology is indistinguishable from
magic.
Clarke's Third Law

Old Friends,

remembered, of times gone by,
when we were young, sometimes wild, and spry.
I've always wondered how you fared?
Did you become stuck,
or what all you dared?
In my later years
I questioned this more.
I tracked some of you down,
and found several gone.
It was a joy to find one or the other,
after fifty years and more,
but there are still some,
I am searching for.
I would love to sit down with you
to talk of what happened,
how we succeeded,
and where we failed.
How we suffered,
and what made us happy,
to share our lives
now almost gone by.

If you lived long enough, you could love all people who are
decent and just . . .
Robert A. Heinlein

Dyed-in-the-Wool Conservatives

want to stop the world.
Their minds are frozen in time.
While values need to be maintained,
times change, technology impacts our lives,
and thus values must be aligned.
What if – we still had slavery
and women without a vote,
no ramps and toilets for handicapped,
and no social security to boot?
Homosexuality, ages old,
swept under the rug,
now in the open,
is still under attack.
Remember you Conservatives of what is said:
"We hold these truths to be self-evident,
that all men are created equal,
endowed by their Creator,
with certain unalienable Rights,
among which are Life, Liberty and the pursuit of Happiness."
The future will bring more changes yet,
life will adjust even more –
behold, it's a certain bet!

A conservative is a man who does not think that anything
should be done for the first time.
Frank Vanderlip

Rationalist

You may wonder
what kind of creature this is
who thinks that reason is in itself
a source of knowledge,
superior and independent of the senses.
So, instead of ideology holding sway,
he holds that reason and experience
rather than non-rational beliefs
are the fundamental criteria
in solving problems.
If people would hearken,
heed more this call,
and with their beliefs
would be less in thrall,
life would be much better
and we would get ahead.
Go tell this to those voting Congress in,
they get who they vote for,
most worth the dust bin.
I beg for reason,
compromise and solution
so that this country
won't face dissolution.

People do not seem to realize that their opinion of the world
is also a confession of character.
Ralph Waldo Emerson

Schmupp

We once had a cat,
the kids brought him in,
a parking lot foundling,
a cute little thing.
He grew and he grew,
was an outdoor cat,
came in for some petting and to sup.
In the evening he settled onto my legs,
stretched out on a footstool, his body relaxed.
I've often claimed that my mother and he
were the only ones
who loved me completely, warts and all.
and I loved him back, as it was my call.
I loved him
by holding still for his stretching,
and when it was called for
took care of his retching.
Then, when he fell sick
and faint wasted away,
I wrapped him in a sheet,
held him tight to my chest,
he feebly struggled,
then was at rest.

When the need arises –
you must be able to shoot your own dog.
Don't farm it out –
that doesn't make it nicer, it makes it worse.
Robert E. Heinlein

Bleeding-Heart Liberals

want it all,
no matter what the cost.
But money doesn't grow on trees,
from the economy come it must.
And if the economy becomes strangulated
by regulational excess,
then there's even less of money
to support the desired largesse.
The poor and deserving should be supported,
our creed does call for it,
but we must always keep in mind
that a balance is called for,
for us to be ever so kind.
And we need to remember
that we must care for ourselves,
and not rely on others,
or the state to simply help.

Democracy is a government where you can say what you think
even if you don't think.
Anonymous

Averto

for the Romans meant:
to avoid, turn back, or turn away.
Now, what are people called
who, with their eyes averted,
simply sweep under the rug
that which they don't want to see?
Lo and behold
there is no word
for this prevalent action
and the people among whom this behavior is shared.
So I had to create one,
for which Latin is good.
I call it avertism
and those who perform it
avertists to boot.

It is well for people who think to change their minds
occasionally
in order to keep them clean....
For those who do not think, it is best at least to rearrange their
prejudices once in a while.
Luther Burbank

Poem

For a poem to come to life
I need motivation,
an inner urge to express an emotion.
It can be joyous, angry or stark,
often it is to leave a mark.
Poems do not arise on command,
they arise from the depth,
from a spirit of mind.

Creativity is allowing yourself to make mistakes. Art is knowing
which ones to keep.
Scott Adams

Impatience

When I was young
I was a dreamer.
It was the hard way
that I learned to get things done.
I became impatient with myself and others,
but learned to temper my demands.
Life thus went on
in breadth and length,
and turned out quite well in the end.
Decisions came as were required,
and I resolved to call
Impatience
my curse but also my strength!

Nobody ever did anything very foolish,
except from some strong principle.
Melbourne

Vanity 2

Vanity, oh vanity,
it creeps up on us sly.
Before we realize
the conceit we hold,
it grows and multiplies.
Oh poet, fellow Man, and reader,
beware and be on guard,
for if awareness of this process fails
and the slippery slope prevails,
sincerity becomes its victim
and falsehood its reward.

People do not seem to realize that their opinion of the world is
also a confession of character.
Ralph Waldo Emerson

Supper

Canoeing the Zambezi River with our guide,
his young wife and some helpers
driving a trail by the river,
set up camp every night.
For three days we paddled,
passing hippos aplenty.
Each evening we found respite, a shower nearby.
One night was special,
forever to behold.
Not far from the river our table was set
with all the accouterments
of civilization one expects.
The mighty, gnarled tree
under which we dined lent character,
held civilization and the wilds entwined.
And on the waters moonlight reflected,
joined by a streak of Venus shine.
On the opposite bank a hyena cackled,
while we eleven in comfort dined.
Some people may see this in a different light,
that it was no adventure but "safari light."
Yet I remember it
as a magical night.

We act as though comfort and luxury are the chief requirements
of life, when all we need to make us really happy is something
to be enthusiastic about.
Charles Kingsley

Lucidity

Years ago when I went to college,
I, with a fellow-student talked,
about a serious problem she had.
We sat in the sunshine after class,
and talked and talked,
but I forgot what the subject was.
What I never forgot
was the fantastic sensation
when I suddenly realized
my heightened awareness,
a lucidity of understanding all.
I then drove home,
but became saddened
once I realized
that my lucidity was gone,
and I had returned to my mental norm.

He that leaveth nothing to chance will do few things ill,
but he will do very few things.
Halifax

Dipper,

water bird it is.
Its nest built precariously,
rushing water beneath.
The veil of a waterfall
makes for a secretive place,
from where it dashes out
to rocks in the creek.
From there it dips and dives in the water
to feed itself and its young,
to rise, then to perch
on a rock again.
It keeps dipping its tail,
which gives it its name,
and to send to the world
a vivacious hail.

The Earth does not belong to us; we belong to the Earth.
Man did not weave the web of life; he is merely a strand in it.
Whatever he does to the web,
he does to himself.
Chief Seattle

Sing

When I was young
I loved to sing.
Jazz was my guide,
its freedom my win.
I sang by myself
but never with others,
oft driving a car
or into the wind,
and the sounds of the sea
were drawing me in.

Happiness lies in the joy of achievement and the thrill of
creative effort.
Franklin D. Roosevelt

Father

was a quiet man.
I called him Papa, as it's done in German.
He did not know a dad himself, why was never told.
His mother raised him – gosh – by knitting
for a living a hundred years ago.
The two must have been poor as hell,
she was a tough one, he as well.
He made his way, became chief engineer.
His sense of humor and demeanor
gained him the liking of his men.
Grown up himself without a father,
he related little with his son,
but left myself free to become,
yet wasn't with his patience shy
for this math-deficient boy.
Once I had grown into my teens,
I learned to tease him by gentle means.
A smile was often the result,
which told me we had found each other.
I never learned what he believed,
but think, I know, he was relieved,
when I, at last, could show him, too,
that I had achieved
– more or less –
what he had hoped for me to do.

Our greatest glory is not in never failing, but in rising up every time we fail.
Ralph Waldo Emerson

Olympic Peninsula

The sky peers through the crowns of giants,
of Hemlock, Douglas Fir and Sitka Spruce,
the rain forests of America's West Coast.
The light is dim and all is quiet,
like in a Gothic church of old.
Veils of Spanish moss drape these survivors,
their storm-tossed comrades on their knees;
nurse logs they are in rot and mold,
enabling youngsters to take hold.
Green scent pervades the air around,
decay, its subtle smell abounds.
And mushrooms, mushrooms everywhere,
to thrive and nourish this biosphere.
Rivulets run here and there
to form a gurgling creek somewhere,
eventually to find the sea,
where clouds return their essence and –
as mist and rain aplenty
are nourishing this magic land.

A little learning is a dangerous thing;
drink deep or taste not the Pierian spring.
Alexander Pope in 'An Essay on Criticism.'

Trauma

There was a time
when I was seven,
in nineteen-forty-four.
The bombings had increased by then.
The day-raids did not cause much fright.
But sirens howling in the night
resulted in the messy plight,
this for myself and for my parents,
that they had need to clean my pants
I'd soiled from hearing the alarms,
before we could resort to shelter.
Much later, in the years to come,
my head jerked up
when in the night
I heard the sound
of four-prop aircraft,
expecting them to drop their bombs.
At least no longer did I soil my pants.
It's only with the start of jets
this wariness I lost
and, in the end, I have to say
that I was luckier than most.

No passion so effectually robs the mind of all its powers of
acting and reasoning as fear.
For fear being an apprehension of pain or death,
it operates in a manner that resembles actual pain.
Edmund Burke

Costa Concordia

Too much went wrong;
stupidity reigned,
too many lives were lost,
but in the end we gained:
The knowledge that we can right a wrong,
by refloating this wreck,
knowing well what we've done.
Many may see it as just one more event,
one more human folly,
something else we rent.
But I cannot help thinking
that in righting this wrong,
we succeeded and showed
that, in the end, we won.

Begin difficult things when they are easy.
Do great things when they are small.
The difficult things of the world must once have been easy.
The great things must once have been small.
A thousand mile journey begins with one step.
Lao Tse

Folly

In our folly, pervasive,
I sometimes rejoice,
the silliness, stupidity, and cruelty,
being our choice.
And yet, at the same time,
I grieve for us,
the turmoil we cause,
our suffering and loss.
I am part of this tapestry,
this richness of life,
the good and the bad,
our joy and strife.
I encompass it all,
the way it is.
We are made for greatness,
but sometimes like beasts
we create a life,
of hell or of heaven,
whose destiny we aren't able to fathom.

What all the wise men promised has not happened,
and what the damned fools said has come to pass.
Melbourne

Bias,

the scourge of our being,
to be beholden by what we believe.
No matter the facts,
"we" know what is right,
"mother's milk" must have done it,
surely, it might.
There is never a weighing,
a skeptical questing,
the beholder remains
in his mental prison.
Were there a creator
who could make them a gift,
it would be that these beholders,
captives in time,
could find a new tune
and a different rhyme.

In the long run, it is better to understand the way the world
really is rather than how we would like it to be.
Michael Shermer

Purpose

Most of my poems are meant to stir the mind,
and better, even the soul.
Ever so subtle,
but sometimes quite bold,
I hope they will come to play a role,
to, maybe, change the reader's perceptions,
to which he's dearly hanging on,
or never entertained before.
It's not my intention to change his mind,
but rather to make him think,
and skeptically evaluate
that which could use
a little jolt or kink.

No rational argument will have a rational effect on a man who
does not want to adopt a rational attitude.
Karl Popper

Cat Haiku

Sinuous feline
with your sharp claws retracted
how blessed I am

Seek simplicity but distrust it.
Alfred N. Whitehead

Limits of Love

When I read from Robert Heinlein's novel
"Time Enough for Love,"
the line that says
"If you'd live long enough,
you could love all those who are decent and just,"
I was told by a Buddhist and a Christian,
that were you truly one,
you could love all people, every single one!
From where I stand
I cannot help saying
that I cannot love a Hitler,
a Wayne Gacy, a Torquemada, a Pol Pot,
or the many more like such.
I am no Buddha or Jesus to boot,
my ability to love
is limited at root.
Thus it is I say – I must,
that I can love only those
"who are decent and just!"

We have become makers of our fate when we have ceased to
pose as its prophets.
Karl Popper

Colorado Heights

A flock of geese honks in the meadows,
some horses take their ease besides.
Across, the cottonwoods begin to yellow,
they hide the river, not its noise.
Its waters rushing to the ocean,
so distant yet so close in mind.
Beyond, the aspen in the foothills yellow,
the rains this year delayed their change
to highlight the dark green of pines.
Forest tongues creep up the mountains,
trees cling tenaciously to ledges,
there nourished by the rain and seepage.
Then, in the distance rise the crags,
the ridges of the Continental Divide,
some dusted by an early snow,
while here, the valley down below,
awaits its winter's load of snow.
I love the peace, the croak of ravens,
wondering what years I'll yet be given
to take this in before it ends and will be riven.

Do not go where the path may lead,
go instead where there is no path and leave a trail.
Ralph Waldo Emerson

Bluebird,

bluebird, of bright color,
fluttering hither and yon.
Sometimes single and sometimes flocking,
you so much brighten life in the sun.

Whoever fights monsters should see to it that in the process he
doesn't become a monster.
Friedrich Wilhelm Nietzsche

Time Spans

At times we are urged to live in the present,
to experience, to savor that which is,
and not to ponder what yet is to be.
While this is important to live life to the fullest,
most people cannot beyond a life span see!
If we truly are to live life to the fullest,
we must also learn to think in thousands,
even in millions of years,
this into the past and into the future,
to fathom the depth of life,
and what – if we are lucky –
is yet to be.

If we have seen further, it is by standing on the shoulders of
giants.
Isaac Newton

Mountain View

White puffs of clouds rise over the mountains,
the sky above pure blue.
Dark green the conifers below,
sprinkled by aspen patches
in their yellow glow.
Soon will this yellow turn to gray,
and winter's snow will cover all,
to rise anew in years to come
for all to see
and – maybe – me.

Adopt the pace of nature: her secret is patience.
Ralph Waldo Emerson

Aspen,

in the autumn light,
your sap diminished, as it might.
Leaves shining in a glorious yellow,
soon turning orange, red and russet,
then growing frost to turn you mellow.
Soon, they will sprinkle the forest floor,
a colorful carpet, more and more,
then fading to dust under winter's snow,
to nourish the life of next year's growth.

Not everything that is faced can be changed, but nothing can
be changed until it is faced.
James Baldwin

Ika

Fifty-seven years ago our paths did cross,
I still a boy of twenty – you, a lady,
most gorgeous to behold, to see.
I quickly changed my views of beauty,
your grace, your poise, taught it to me.
I had to overcome initial hesitation
to make you leave my father's car into your home.
I am delighted that you set my standards
of what a woman ought to be.
And while you were like Ingmar Bergman's movie,
"A Summer's time she only danced,"
our all too brief encounter set me free.
Since such a classy lady as you had accepted me,
there was a world now to explore and conquer,
and although it did take awhile,
I realized my dreams and made them come to be.
Here I now sit in Colorado's heights at seventy-seven,
while you, an ocean and a life apart,
will celebrate your eightieth birth
to which I wish you a most
Happy Birthday, Ika,
this, from the bottom of my heart.
May you stay hale and sound for years to come,
and sometimes ponder, how live's paths cross – part,
yet in the memory live on.

When one door closes another door opens;
but we often look so long and so regretfully upon the closed
door that we do not see the ones which open for us.
Alexander Graham Bell

Manhood

like womanhood, changes through time,
depending on technology and culture,
it's without reason or rhyme.
But whatever its expressions,
its cultural traits,
the capacity to be human
should never fail.
To be strong, yet to feel,
and whenever it's right,
to let know of these feelings
whatever they might.

Science must begin with myths, and with the criticism of myths.
Karl Popper

Frozen

What I am saying and try to do
is to stir the mind, be skeptical,
raise one's awareness,
check one's bias.
Yet I have found increasingly
that, even when done teasingly
or gently if called for,
when a dearly held belief is challenged,
the holder tightly clings to it,
refuses to see and to find relief,
and in denial remains the eternal captive
unaware of his frozen belief.

The mark of a first-rate intelligence is the ability to hold
contradictory ideas in the mind at the same time and still
function.
Scott Fitzgerald

Exceptionalism

"We hold these Truths to be self-evident . . ."
The founders of this Great Nation declared.
And would you believe it,
today, few of its people are aware of what it means.
Yet it is at the base of this nation,
the belief being held
that "we are better than them,"
than the rest of the world with all its mayhem.
Many hold the belief that "we don't need them" at all,
a mistaken belief that keeps them in thrall. –
There once was a nation many centuries ago
whose elites justly thought the same, also.
The Chinese Empire, greatest producer of world GDP,
rich and secure, controlled its environs and its sea.
Her elites and her emperor justly thought
that, exceptional, their nation was greatest,
the world's rest did not count.
But it didn't take long for the Western upstarts
to badger her down at her shores.
Beware you elites
who think yourselves exceptional:
all exceptionalism is transitory,
and will end on the scrap pile of history.

There is no history of mankind, there are only many histories of all kinds of
aspects of human life. And one of these is the history of political power.
This is elevated into the history of the world.
Karl Popper

Limits of Knowledge

Whatever there is
that cannot be known,
should not be dealt with,
should be left to its own.
But if you find pleasure
to toy with such things
that are without reason or rhyme,
then wallow in it,
but be aware that down here in the ditches
are things to attend to,
with many more urgent,
some more sublime.

Insofar as a scientific statement speaks about reality, it must be falsifiable; and insofar as it is not falsifiable, it does not speak about reality.
Karl Popper

Civilization

Among many things civilization provides
are the rules and customs we are asked to abide.
We must keep this in mind
when venturing forth
in trying to change them,
put new ones in place.
There's a reason for civilization's demands,
established through time
and proven to work
even when some feel
a call for repeal.
From time to time some certainly do,
but we should beware
when we improvise rules
that they maintain civilization,
not diminish or wreck it,
and keep it alive.

Horror is the law of the world of living creatures,
and civilization is concerned with masking the truth.
Czeslaw Milosz in Anus Mundi

Metaphysics

The pantheon of gods
the Ancients worshipped
eventually became worn,
as do all human creations,
after a thousand year turn.
Thus, twenty centuries ago,
plenty of new beliefs
vied for people's attention,
and kept them in sway,
until a couple, after quite some struggle,
left all others behind
to become dominant to this day.
Now, one is fading,
at least in some quarters,
we are back where we were
two-thousand years later.
People are searching to fill the void.
Thus the search is on for what else be there.
Metaphysics is what lies beyond objective experience,
meaning, some of what people come up with is fine,
however, much which these days is "created," promoted,
is out of this world,
doesn't hold water,
nor does it shine.

It is impossible to communicate to people who have not experienced it
the undefinable menace of total rationalism.
Czeslaw Milosz

Phenotype

There is a man
half black, half white,
his external appearance
called the phenotype.
Yet internally, his genotype,
one half is black the other white!
But because his features
look more black than white,
he's classified as Black,
but not as White!
And a woman,
the offspring of an Asian and White,
is she called Asian,
would that be right?
People, oh people,
what's in a name,
why must we peg people?
It is such a shame!
Why can it simply not be enough?
– we are one species –
then call us such.
No matter the features of woman or man,
call us and act what we are –
Human!

To err is human; to forgive, divine.
Alexander Pope

Dedication

There's a certain young couple,
I have seen at the YMCA for years.
She is bound to a wheelchair,
can barely get up.
With exquisite care
he helps her on and off the machines,
while she then pursues her varied regimes.
I could not help but admire this pair.
So, after many times of thinking it,
I finally told them:
"Allow me to say
with my greatest respect,
I admire your dedication."
This was it.
I just had to tell them
– they looked up at me –
Was there love in their eyes?
Did I properly see?

We gain strength, and courage, and confidence by each
experience in which we really stop to look fear in the face ... we
must do that which we think we cannot.
Eleanor Roosevelt

Fall

Once more leaves are turning,
their colors rich, brown, yellow, and red.
The winds now fresh and bolder
make them dance, then tumble to the ground.
Their mold'ring scent,
rich to inhale,
contributes to this season's tale.
A nip of frost is in the air,
the jays stash seeds,
their winter's fare.
The days grow shorter,
nights get longer,
the mornings call for extended slumber.
A sweater, too, is now in order,
yet, for as long as there is sun,
then day by day,
the winter's snow is held at bay.

At the entrance, my bare feet on the dirt floor.
Here, gusts of heat; at my back, white clouds.
I stare and stare. It seems I was called for this: To glorify things
just because they are.
Czeslaw Milosz

Dissociation

What is it that's happening,
near and far,
the acts of violence
against people, animals, objects and Nature,
committed by those
who don't seem to care,
who lack a sense of belonging,
as it were?
These acts perpetrated
by individuals and groups
are indicative of their non-integration,
of their lack of awareness, of education.
The more people there are,
the lesser the association.
But what's missing most
is comprehension of their actions,
and the consequences of their dissociation.

What is poetry which does not save nations or people?
Czeslaw Milosz

Oneness

Those who commit mayhem and murder,
hurt, destroy and wreck Nature,
have something in common
in that they lack oneness,
the sense of belonging
to a larger whole,
the association of Man.
Oft are they loners,
at most gathered in groups,
yet all miss the sense
of unity, and hence
perpetrate these acts of violence
against the society
wherin they exist.
They have no respect,
they couldn't care less,
because they lack
what I call oneness.

A hundred times every day I remind myself that my inner and
outer life depends on the labors of other men, living and dead,
and that I must exert myself in order to give in the measure as I
have received and am still receiving.

Albert Einstein

Bush Walk

I have been on treks through Africa's bush,
across her savannas, along her rivers and such.
The guide in the lead,
his charges single file in tow,
sometimes a guard with a rifle ahead of the row.
Along the walk you never know
what to expect or what you'll see.
Cape buffalo may hide in the bush,
a hippo may just leave a pond,
elephants beside a tree may stand.
Benign it is to meet an impala herd,
to come across some elephant turds,
their cellulose still food for termites make.
This is an experience I wouldn't miss,
to be part of the wilds,
knowingly vulnerable, it is.
For there, too, are lions,
You just never know.
Do enjoy this experience
but remain on your toes,
as everyone who has taken a bush walk knows.

The risk of a wrong decision is preferable to the terror of
indecision.
Maimonides

Belief 2

People are able to believe
in just about anything there is,
what they imagine and create,
and what as truth they then do state.
Be these entrails of goats, or witches,
sea monsters, ghosts, and UFOs,
gods and goddesses and fairies,
whatever comes into Man's mind.
Can then not God be far behind?

Whenever a theory appears to you as the only possible one,
take this as a sign that you have neither understood the theory
nor the problem which it was intended to solve.
Karl Popper

Consciousness 2

Conciousness, our glory and terror,
root of conscience and morals,
so prone to error.
Evolved through millennia,
even millions of years,
it raised us from apes
to the status of Man.
With it we created
the arts, the sciences, and engineering,
to control our world.
Will it go on?
Will we yet learn
to keep emotions in check,
not to suppress them
but to save our neck?
For we are in trouble,
as a species goes.
Let us work on and hope
we'll overcome our woes.

I think we have all experienced passion that is not in any sense
reasonable.
Stephen Fry

Magnificence

When we observe what men and women,
hale or impaired, these days perform,
we must marvel at what we, as a species, can do.
We are pushing the limits
ever farther beyond
that which is normal,
on air, sea and land.
What is it that drives us to take on such risks,
to excel in these tasks and daring?
What is it we're trying to prove to the world?
Is it the intensity of living beheld?
While I'm not as daring as many are,
I am part of this species
and proud so to be.
Are some of us simply saying we can,
that we try and succeed,
sometimes fail
to meet our death knell?
So, with all the trouble we create,
still, it must be said:
What a magnificent species we make!

What you haven't got in your head,
you've got to have in your legs.
Hans Windolf

Mistakes

To tell the truth, I've made a few,
in the course of my many years.
All, though, go back to an earlier age,
when still young I was learning what goes.
Some small, others large,
the small ones serving to learn,
some of the large ones made me yearn
not to have made them,
but it is too late,
one cannot reverse what once was made.
So I must live with what I have done,
the good and the bad,
on that final run,
hope that my failures
will be forgiven
in the years that are yet to come.

There is no doubt that in exchanging a self-centered for a
selfless life we gain enormously in self-esteem.
The vanity of the selfless, even those who practice utmost
humility, is boundless.
Eric Hoffer

Life 2

Since time immemorial
we have tried and tried
to make life secure, and to avoid
what Nature's vagaries throw our way.
Prevent, we have some,
but it's never enough.
The forces of Nature will test us forever
and wreck peoples' lives
as if they were chaff.
Haiyan, the typhoon,
just showed us again
that we must stand together
to recover, to win.
Then, there are people
who, without much sense,
do fight against Man,
from whatever their creed,
while they don't seem to know
that there is this great force,
Nature, it's called,
that threatens life more,
against which we should rally
for success and succor.

Man: the glory, jest, and riddle of the world.
Alexander Pope

Marvel

What marvels we are,
it is hard to behold.
Lots of water,
some minerals,
and bacteria aplenty
we do hold.
With such little substance
we can ponder the world
and marvel
about our very selves.

Not everything that is faced can be changed, but nothing can
be changed until it is faced.
James Baldwin

Deep Time 2

Deep Time, so difficult to comprehend,
the millions of years
that are by it meant.
The millions of species
which swam the seas,
the many more which walked the land.
Then not to forget,
the deserts, the mountains,
the seas that were rent.
So ephemeral we are,
we just cannot fathom
the eons of time,
passed before we arrived,
and those yet to come
when we are no longer alive.

Death is natural and our biggest problem is our fear of it.
Seneca

Mother

was, what in Yiddish is called,
a Mensch.
A simple woman,
she worked all her life,
yet provided for others at length.
Troubled and ill in her later years,
she found some libations to still her tears.
But when her time came
she did not delay,
and left this world
in the blink of an eye.

All Nature is but art, unknown to thee;
All chance, direction, which thou canst not see;
All discord, harmony not understood;
And spite of pride, in erring reason's spite,
One truth is clear; whatever is, is right.
Alexander Pope
"Essay on Man, from Epistle I"

Respect

*I do not have heroes
but there are a few men
for whom I have great respect.
Lewis and Clark, and Shackelton,
who explored, suffered and accomplished,
and brought all their men back!*

Do not go where the path may lead,
go instead where there is no path and leave a trail.
Ralph Waldo Emerson

Sail on

Were there one more life,
I would love to sail
the seas of the world
with the tiniest crew
I'd be able to hail.
I wonder about the ocean's call,
when in this life I was no seaman at all.
But the sea feels eternal,
and what little I saw,
sunrises and sunsets
are on sea without par.
Alas, I don't bicker,
I am content,
enough time allowed,
far along in the future,
I'll return to her depths
when once more, given time,
she will conquer the land.

It is desirable for a man to be blotted out at his proper time.
For as nature has marked the bounds of everything else, so
she has marked the bounds of life. Moreover, old age is the
final scene, as it were, in life's drama, from which we ought to
escape when it grows wearisome and, certainly, when we have
had our fill.
Cicero

Testament

To come to the end:
This is where I stand!
With all that I've missed,
mistook and beheld.

The time has come, the walrus said, to talk of many things; of
shoes and ships and sealing wax, of cabbages and kings, and
why the sea is boiling hot,
and whether pigs have wings.
Lewis Carrol

Spirit

by Karl May

It was the day the spirit woke,
from waters, dreaming of worlds far removed,
reflecting on the word of the Almighty God,
from which his wondrous promise to him spoke:

I grant you now this image: Earth.
Go there, humanely make it come to be,
so that through love, divine it shall become,
which, from my Father's house, I do send on.

Then, in the east, the light of lights took hold,
life's tide, which everlasting blooms,
and full of wonder was he face-to-face,
the spirit - for the first time - with the face of God.

If

by Rudyard Kipling

If you can keep your head when all about you are losing theirs and
blaming it on you;

If you can trust yourself when all men doubt you, but
make allowance for their doubting too;

If you can wait and not be tired of waiting, or, being lied about, don't
deal in lies, or being hated don't give way to hating, and yet don't
look too good, nor talk too wise;

If you can dream - and not make dreams your master;

If you can think - and not make thoughts your aim;

If you can meet with Triumph and Disaster and treat those two
impostors just the same;

If you can bear to have the truth you've spoken twisted by knaves
to make a trap for fools, or watch the things you gave your life to,
broken, and stoop and build 'em up with worn out tools;

If you can make one heap of all your winnings and risk it on one turn
of pitch-and-toss, and lose, and start again at your beginnings, and
never breathe a word about your loss;

If you can force your heart and nerve and sinew to serve your turn long after they are gone, and so hold on when there is nothing in you except the Will which says to them "Hold on!"

If you can talk with crowds and keep your virtue, or walk with Kings - nor lose the common touch;

If neither foes nor loving friends can hurt you;

If all men count with you, but none too much;

If you can fill the unforgiving minute with sixty seconds' worth of distance run, Yours is the Earth and everything that's in it.

And - which is more - you'll be a man, my son!

Observations
and
Reflections

by Herbert Windolf

ISBN: 1494432951
ISBN 13: 9781494432959